SpringerBriefs in Public Health

SpringerBriefs in Public Health present concise summaries of cutting-edge research and practical applications from across the entire field of public health, with contributions from medicine, bioethics, health economics, public policy, biostatistics, and sociology.

The focus of the series is to highlight current topics in public health of interest to a global audience, including health care policy; social determinants of health; health issues in developing countries; new research methods; chronic and infectious disease epidemics; and innovative health interventions.

Featuring compact volumes of 50 to 125 pages, the series covers a range of content from professional to academic. Possible volumes in the series may consist of timely reports of state-of-the art analytical techniques, reports from the field, snapshots of hot and/or emerging topics, elaborated theses, literature reviews, and in-depth case studies. Both solicited and unsolicited manuscripts are considered for publication in this series.

Briefs are published as part of Springer's eBook collection, with millions of users worldwide. In addition, Briefs are available for individual print and electronic purchase.

Briefs are characterized by fast, global electronic dissemination, standard publishing contracts, easy-to-use manuscript preparation and formatting guidelines, and expedited production schedules. We aim for publication 8–12 weeks after acceptance.

More information about this series at http://www.springer.com/series/10138

Chris Chanyasulkit

Successful Public Health Advocacy

Lessons Learned from Massachusetts Legislators

With Contributions by Georges C. Benjamin, Jennifer Childs-Roshak, Stefanie Coxe, Cynthia Creem, Julie Graves, and Tricia Wajda

 Springer

Chris Chanyasulkit
Brookline, MA, USA

ISSN 2192-3698   ISSN 2192-3701   (electronic)
SpringerBriefs in Public Health
ISBN 978-3-030-30286-3   ISBN 978-3-030-30288-7   (eBook)
https://doi.org/10.1007/978-3-030-30288-7

This Springer imprint is published by the registered company Springer Nature Switzerland AG
The registered company address is: Gewerbestrasse 11, 6330 Cham, Switzerland

This monograph is dedicated to Hunter Christopher Bardin, Grayson James Bardin, Genevieve Rose Bardin, and James William Bardin.

Preface

Racial and ethnic disparities in health are a major concern for citizens, states, and our nation and are important to study and understand to strategically address and eliminate such inequities. This brief is designed to share the lessons learned from an exploratory study in which key legislators from the Massachusetts General Court (legislature) were interviewed to determine their level of awareness and knowledge regarding health disparities. From these lessons, public health advocates can better understand whether and how factors affect knowledge and awareness of health disparities to more effectively communicate with legislators, key stakeholders, and other decision-makers. Using data on how legislators gather their health information for policymaking or constituent work will assist advocates in determining how to best communicate their message and successfully advocate for their causes.

In addition to data from interview research, this brief provides advocates with "Notes from the Field" from those experts working in the "trenches" to provide firsthand advice for advocates in the hopes of closing the disparities gaps and creating a more equitable nation for all.

Brookline, MA, USA   Chris Chanyasulkit

Acknowledgments

Many thanks to Janet Kim, Khristine Queja, and the Springer team for their support, encouragement, and guidance. Special thanks also to Dr. Georges C. Benjamin of the American Public Health Association, Dr. Jennifer Childs-Roshak and Tricia Wajda of the Planned Parenthood Advocacy Fund of Massachusetts, Stefanie Coxe of Nexus Werx, Dr. Julie Graves of Nurx, and Senator Cynthia Stone Creem of the Massachusetts legislature who each provide key insight for influencing policymakers. Final thanks also to Michael S. Dukakis for continuing to inspire me and so many to think about public service and politics. Michael S. Dukakis is distinguished professor of Political Science at Northeastern University and a visiting professor at the Luskin School of Public Affairs at the UCLA. He was the three-term governor of Massachusetts and the 1988 democratic nominee for president of the United States. His leadership, research, and advocacy on national health-care policy reform, his continued political activism in Massachusetts, and his encouragement of grassroots organizing continue to inspire students, activists, and myself.

Contents

**1 Health Disparities: What Are "Health Disparities"?
Why Do We Care? Should We Care?**   1
Introduction.   5
Public Health and Politics.   6
Becoming the Chief Health Strategist.   7
Advocacy   8
Coalition Building.   9
Conclusion   9
References.   9

**2 "The More You Know, the Further You'll Go" or What Do
Legislators Know About Health Disparities and What Does
This Mean for Public Health Advocates?** 11
Notes in the Field 11
References. 22

3 How to Get Your Legislator's Attention 23
Introduction. 26
Building Relationships and Political Capital 26
Building Relationships 27
Building Political Capital 27
The Anatomy of the Ask. 29
Decide What the *Specific Ask* Is 29
Do Your Homework 30
Effective Messaging 30
The One-Pager or "Leave-Behind" Document. 31
Get on Their Schedule. 32
Perfect Your Elevator Speech 32
Follow-Up, Follow-Up, Follow-Up 33
Conclusion 33
References. 34

4   If at First You Don't Succeed............................... 35
The Planned Parenthood Advocacy Fund of Massachusetts'
Legislative Priorities in the 2017–2018 Legislative Agenda............. 37
Our 2017–2018 Legislative Successes Included: 38
Best Practices for Legislative Advocacy.......................... 39
Conclusion 42
References... 43

Appendix A: Interview Questions for Legislators 45

Index... 51

Endorsement

"I have known Chris Chanyasulkit since she was a graduate student of mine at Northeastern University – and she was a fine one. What's more, she has continued to be a public advocate, as a teacher, and as an elected official in our hometown. And she won that office the old-fashioned way – house to house and door to door. When it comes to public advocacy, she knows whereof she speaks."

– Michael S. Dukakis, JD, Former Governor of Massachusetts
and Distinguished Professor of Political Science
at Northeastern University

About the Author

Chris Chanyasulkit, PhD, MPH is grounded in a strong belief in eliminating the structural barriers to equity for vulnerable populations. She previously served as a gubernatorial appointee to both the Massachusetts Asian American Commission and the Commission on the Status of Women. In that capacity, she advocated for the needs of Asian Americans and women throughout the Commonwealth. She has served as the Assistant Director of the Brookline Office of Diversity, Inclusion, and Community Relations and continues to teach and lecture in universities throughout Boston.

After earning her BA from Boston University, with dual majors in biology and art history, she joined AmeriCorps and assisted nonprofits in developing and maintaining technological competency in the administration and delivery of services. Following that, she returned to Boston University and completed a master's degree in public health (concentrating in maternal and child health care). After graduating, she worked in the Department of Immunology and Infectious Diseases at the Harvard T.H. Chan School of Public Health. She also holds a doctoral degree in political science, with a concentration in public policy, from Northeastern University, where she conducted research on health disparities.

In addition to her advocacy and scholarly pursuits, she is an elected trustee of the Public Libraries of Brookline, a Brookline Town Meeting member, a Brookline Community Emergency Response Team member, a Brookline Medical Reserve Corps member, and a mentor mom for Beth Israel Deaconess Medical Center's Parent Connection Program among other civic engagements. With a proven public health background, she was elected to the Executive Board of the American Public Health Association and currently serves as its vice-chair. She is also an appointed member of the US Department of Health and Human Services Regional Health Equity Council for New England. When she is not advocating for public health policies, you can likely find her running around one of Brookline's many parks with her husband and three young children.

About the Contributors

Georges Benjamin, MD is known as one of the nation's most influential physician leaders because he speaks passionately and eloquently about health issues having the most impact on our nation today. From his firsthand experience as a physician, he knows what happens when preventive care is not available and when the healthy choice is not the easy choice. As executive director of the American Public Health Association (APHA) since 2002, he is leading the Association's push to make America the healthiest nation in one generation.

He came to the APHA from his position as secretary of the Maryland Department of Health and Mental Hygiene. He became secretary of health in Maryland in April 1999, following 4 years as its deputy secretary for public health services. As secretary, he oversaw the expansion and improvement of the state's Medicaid program.

He, of Gaithersburg, Maryland, is a graduate of the Illinois Institute of Technology and the University of Illinois College of Medicine. He is board-certified in internal medicine and a fellow of the American College of Physicians and the National Academy of Public Administration, a fellow emeritus of the American College of Emergency Physicians, and an honorary fellow of the Royal Society of Public Health.

An established administrator, author, and orator, he started his medical career in 1981 in Tacoma, Washington, where he managed a 72,000 patient visit ambulatory care service as chief of the Acute Illness Clinic at the Madigan Army Medical Center and was an attending physician within the Department of Emergency Medicine. A few years later, he moved to Washington, DC, where he served as chief of Emergency Medicine at the Walter Reed Army Medical Center. After leaving the Army, he chaired the Department of Community Health and Ambulatory Care at the District of Columbia General Hospital. He was promoted to acting commissioner for public health for the District of Columbia and later directed one of the busiest ambulance services in the nation as interim director of the Emergency Ambulance Bureau of the District of Columbia Fire Department.

At the APHA, he also serves as publisher of the nonprofit's monthly publication, *The Nation's Health*, the association's official newspaper, and the *American Journal of Public Health*, the profession's premier scientific publication. He is the author of more than 100 scientific articles and book chapters. His recent book *The Quest for Health Reform: A Satirical History* is an exposé of the nearly 100-year quest to ensure quality affordable health coverage for all through the use of political cartoons.

He is a member of the National Academy of Medicine (formerly the Institute of Medicine) of the National Academies of Sciences, Engineering, and Medicine and also serves on the boards for many organizations including Research!America and the Reagan-Udall Foundation. In 2008, 2014, and 2016, he was named one of the top 25 minority executives in health care by *Modern Healthcare* magazine, in addition to being voted among the 100 most influential people in health care from 2007 to 2017.

In April 2016, President Obama appointed him to the National Infrastructure Advisory Council, a council that advises the president on how best to assure the security of the nation's critical infrastructure.

Jennifer Childs-Roshak, MD, MBA is president and CEO of Planned Parenthood League of Massachusetts and president of Planned Parenthood Advocacy Fund of Massachusetts. As president and CEO of Planned Parenthood League of Massachusetts, she leads the largest freestanding reproductive health-care provider in the Commonwealth. Every year, PPLM provides a wide range of sexual and reproductive health care to over 30,000 patients across Massachusetts and educates over 12,000 young people, parents, and professionals through PPLM's nationally recognized sexual health education programs. PPLM's *Get Real: Comprehensive Sex Education That Works* curriculum has reached over 217,000 youth and is on the US Department of Health and Human Services list of evidence-based programs. She also serves as the president of the Planned Parenthood Advocacy Fund of Massachusetts, the advocacy and political arm of PPLM. She is the first physician to lead these organizations in their histories.

Her interest in sexual and reproductive health care dates back to her time as a new Harvard graduate working as an editor at the United Nations Fund for Population Activities. Inspired by the work at the UNFPA to ensure universal access to reproductive health, she also volunteered with Planned Parenthood NYC at that time. Together, these experiences motivated her to pursue a career in primary care medicine.

Prior to joining PPLM in November 2015, she served as the Boston Regional Medical director for Atrius Health while personally caring for 1000 patients as a primary care physician. She also served as the site medical director of the Kenmore practice.

She received her medical degree from Temple University School of Medicine in Philadelphia; completed her internship and residency at Maine Medical Center in Portland, Maine; and is board-certified in family medicine. In addition to being a family physician, her leadership roles have included serving as medical director of Quality and department chairperson at the Milford Regional Medical Center and vice president of Medical Services of the Family Health Center of Worcester. She has also served as a faculty physician at the Maine Medical Center Family Medicine, the UMass Family Medicine, and most recently the Brigham and Women's Internal Medicine resident training programs. Complementing her medical degree, she holds a Master of Business Administration from the Boston University School of Management. She and her husband, Phillip Roshak, CPA, have two grown sons and live in Boston.

She is a member of the Massachusetts Medical Society's Physician Health Services Board of Directors. She also serves on various councils focused on improving access to health care.

Stefanie Coxe is the owner of Nexus Werx LLC, an activism and lobbying training and consulting company, and a former legislative staffer. She designs civic engagement programs and offers Learn to Lobby in-person and online courses on lobbying and activism.

She received her B.A. in Legal Education and Economics from the University of Massachusetts Boston and has over 15 years of combined political and nonprofit experience, including serving as an aide to two Massachusetts state representatives and a U.S. congressman.

You can email her at Stefanie@nexuswerx.com or follow her on social media at @learntolobby.

Senator Cynthia Stone Creem has served in a public capacity for more than 30 years, first as a member and president of the Newton Board of Aldermen and then as a member of the Governor's Council prior to becoming State Senator in 1999.

Among her top priorities since entering the Legislature, she has been the leading advocate for restoring judicial discretion in sentencing and eliminating across-the-board mandatory minimum sentences and for increasing safeguards for gun ownership. She has served in a leadership role on many high-profile issues, including a landmark law legalizing stem-cell research, which also boosted our state's biotech economy, and the law that preserves marriage equality, advocating for the bottle bill expansion, energy conservation, and renewable energy, and successfully sponsoring legislation on food allergies.

While chair of the Criminal Justice Committee from 1999 to 2003, she successfully opposed the reinstatement of the death penalty, helped create safety buffer zones around health clinics, and reformed the sex offender registry and the state's drunken driving laws. From 2003 to 2008, as chair of the Revenue Committee, she worked to close corporate tax loopholes and served on a commission whose recommendations were enacted to promote economic growth and benefit Massachusetts companies.

As Senate chair of the Joint Committee on Judiciary from 2009 to 2013, she successfully shepherded legislation reforming the Probation Department, modernizing alimony laws and criminal history records, securing the right to DNA testing in criminal cases, and enacting sentencing reform to save money and reduce recidivism. In 2013–2014, as chair of Senate Post-Audit and Oversight, she issued three reports which led to legislation addressing issues uncovered during the research phase on the handling of rape kits by state agencies, a review of state boards and commissions, and the contracting procedures for information technology projects.

During the 2017–2018 session, as one of the three Senate members on the Criminal Justice House-Senate Conference Committee, she was able to help secure important reforms to the state's policies – reducing the number of crimes susceptible to a mandatory minimum sentence, adding oversight and time limits to solitary confinement of inmates, and moving juveniles and others charged with low-level offenses into diversion programs, including drug and alcohol addiction treatment.

Currently, as majority leader, she places a high priority on issues including criminal justice reform, health care, energy, environment, women's issues, civil rights, education, and revenue.

She and her husband, Harvey, live in Newton and enjoy spending free time with their two children and four grandchildren.

Julie Graves is a family medicine and public health physician who serves as associate director of Clinical Services for Nurx and is associate professor of Family Medicine at Georgetown University School of Medicine and adjunct associate professor of Policy, Management, and Community Health at the University of Texas School of Public Health. She earned her BA in Biology/Physical Education from Rice University, her MD from the University of Texas Southwestern Medical School, and her MPH and PhD from the University of Texas School of Public Health. She completed an internship in general surgery at Parkland Memorial Hospital, trained in anesthesiology at the University of Florida, and completed residency in family medicine at St. Paul Medical Center in Dallas and then a fellowship in faculty development at the McLennan County Medical Education and Research Foundation in Waco, Texas.

She has taught in family medicine, occupational medicine, and preventive medicine residency programs; has taught public health, medical, nursing, and midwifery students; and has developed clinical practice guidelines for medical organizations and government. She served as medical consultant to the Texas Department of Health in infectious diseases epidemiology and surveillance, Medicaid, WIC, and Title V programs and as investigator and monitor for the Texas Medical Board. As medical services coordinator for the Texas Department of Aging and Disability Services, she led quality improvements of medical care in state facilities for people with disabilities and then served as regional medical director for the Texas Department of State Health Services for the Houston area. She has served in leadership positions in the Harris County Medical Society, the Texas Medical Association, the Texas Academy of Family Physicians, the American Medical Association Resident Physicians section, and the American Public Health Association. She has published numerous medical journal articles and textbook chapters and is a fellow of the American Academy of Family Physicians. She was awarded the C. Frank Webber Award for Excellence in Oncology from the University of Texas MD Anderson Cancer Center and the Texas Academy of Family Physicians, has served on the Board of Directors for the Texas Medical Association Political Action

Committee, and has practiced medicine in Texas; Florida; Washington, DC; Maryland; Wisconsin; Germany; and Sint Maarten and on a cruise ship.

Tricia Wajda serves as Vice President of External Affairs of Planned Parenthood Advocacy Fund. She joined Planned Parenthood League of Massachusetts in January 2011 after extensive work in the policy and political arenas. She began her professional career working on reproductive health issues on Capitol Hill for Congresswoman Lynn Woolsey. Prior to coming to PPLM, she served as a senior communications and policy advisor to Michael Flaherty's campaign for the Boston City Council (2007) and Boston mayoral campaign (2009). In addition to leading the organization's government relations, communications, and political organizing, she manages the board, operations, and programming of the Planned Parenthood Advocacy Fund (PPAF), PPLM's political organization. The highlights of her PPLM/PPAF tenure include work responding to the loss of the state's buffer zone and advocacy for the Safe Access Law, the election of Senator Warren, the passage of the Contraceptive Access Law, impactful Sexual Health Lobby Days, and last-minute rallies mobilizing against national "defunding" threats and other attacks on health care. She earned her Masters from American University's School of Public Affairs and currently resides in Needham with her husband John and her three sons, Jack, Elliot, and Finley.

Chapter 1
Health Disparities: What Are "Health Disparities"? Why Do We Care? Should We Care?

Much has been written about this term, "health disparities," and yet, I would venture to say that your average person on the street wouldn't know what you were referring to if you started talking to them about health disparities. But, it's critically important, especially today, that your average person knows about health disparities, cares about them, and works tirelessly to end these differences, for a whole host reasons that we will look at more closely. Health disparities refers to the differences in health and health care that are observed among different racial and ethnic groups, and are a real and major concern in the United States (or at least it should be) and are important to study and address as such disparities affect the overall health and well-being of everyone in the nation. (Williams and Jackson 2005).

Are these health differences small? Are they real? The differences are not small and are very real, especially for those who suffer from poor health outcomes. The following startling health statistics reveal that indeed, health disparities are real, would surprise many policymakers and members of the public and continue to underscore the importance of eliminating health disparities:

- Life expectancy is often thought of as a good indicator of the overall health of a nation so it is sobering to see that according to the National Center for Health Statistics, life expectancy in the U.S. continues to decline (Murphy et al. 2018). Black-white disparities in life expectancy continue to persist, with black adults continuing to have a lower life expectancy than white adults (Health Resources and Services Administration 2018). As of 2015, the life expectancy of a black man at birth was 72.2 years, more than 4 years shorter than that of a white man (American Public Health Association. All Health is Connected: Can Leveraging Women's Health Care Help Narrow Gaps in Black Men's Health?).
- HIV prevalence among blacks is greater than for all other racial/ethnic groups (Herbst et al. 2014).
- It's not just American tennis champion Serena Williams who almost died while giving birth to her daughter, but the case for many black women across this nation. Though global maternal mortality has dropped by almost half over the

last 25 years, black women in the U.S. are still three to four times more likely than non-Hispanic white women to die as a result of giving birth (Creanga et al. 2017).

- African-American infants are 2.5 times more likely to die as infants than non-Hispanic white infants (Mathews and MacDorman 2013).
- Latino adults are 63% more likely to be diabetic than non-Hispanic white adults (Centers for Disease Control and Prevention 2017) and when compared with whites, all major racial/ethnic minority groups had significantly higher diabetes prevalence (Centers for Disease Control and Prevention 2017).
- Communities of color have a 28% higher health burden from air pollution when compared to the overall population and African-Americans face a 54% higher health burden from air pollution when compared to the overall population (Mikati et al. 2018).
- Drug-induced death rates were highest among American Indian/Alaska Natives and non-Hispanic whites (Mack 2013).
- Despite substantial declines in HIV/AIDS mortality since 1987, HIV/AIDS is still the sixth leading cause of death among blacks aged 20–54 years. As recently as 2014, HIV/AIDS mortality was 9.6 times higher among blacks and 2.2 times higher among Hispanics compared to whites (Kochanek 2016).
- Income is a strong influence on where people live, their ability to access to resources, and their ability to engage in healthy behaviors. Since the 1970s, income inequality in the United States has continued to rise with economic and social consequences that are being felt in communities across the nation. A 2018 Pew Research Center study revealed that while the black-white income gaps closed somewhat from 1970 to 2016, Hispanics continued to fall further behind at all income levels. Their research showed that even at the high end of the income distribution, Hispanics earned only 65% as much as whites in 2016 compared with 74% in 1970 (Pew Research Center 2018).
- Poverty data further shows the stark differences in income as related to race/ethnicity. 2015 U.S. Census Bureau data reveal two times higher poverty rates among American Indians/Alaska Natives [AIANs] (26.6%), black/African-Americans (25.4%), Hispanics (22.6%), and Native Hawaiians and other Pacific Islanders (18.9%), when compared with non-Hispanic whites (10.4%) (US Census Bureau 2016). The steady increase in the income inequality continues to influence how communities of color access health resources and engage in healthy behaviors.

The statistics are numbers, but those numbers represent people and lives lost. We should deem them as unacceptable statistics and begin a concerted effort to move others to care about health disparities. If others do not find these statistics unacceptable, they need to realize that as with most things, helping others will help themselves.

It is important for everyone and not only public health practitioners to realize that diseases in smaller communities of color and low socio-economic groups, if left untreated, tend to spread to larger, wealthier populations over time. Furthermore, diseases associated with racial/ethnic health disparities will affect productive capacities and outputs of adults, which can further affect productivity levels at a state and national level. This could lead to a subsequent decrease in tax revenues and increase the cost and use of social services. Additionally, as racial and ethnic groups continue to grow and become a larger percentage of the population, their health care will substantially affect the health of the nation as a whole. Finally, as a matter of social justice, it is important to ensure that all individuals in the health system, regardless of race or ethnicity, are treated adequately and equally. Unfortunately, these statistics and a belief in social justice are still not compelling enough for most of America to take notice and work to close the disparity gaps. But, we must continue to work for change. We cannot accept this as the status quo. We must continue to strive to build a better society that treats everyone equally and that doesn't let the color of your skin or your zip code dictate your future.

What do I mean by "zip code" dictating your future? No, that's not a typo. I didn't mean to write "genetic code." I really did mean "zip code." Your zip code can determine your health and therefore, your future in ways that most people don't think about. Scientists have long studied the genetics component to many diseases and while we know that many genetic diseases are multifactorial, one's environment contributes substantially to one's health and the variations that are seen in the incidence of mortality and morbidity. Budrys notes that "genetic differences explain about 49% of heritability and 51% is explained by the influence of environmental conditions on gene expression" (Budrys 2017). This is important because our environment and many economic and social factors determine one's health. Most public health practitioners refer to this concept as the "social determinants of health." It's the concept that where you live, work, and play affect your health. For example, living in mold-infested housing can be harmful to your health. Some evidence suggests that indoor mold exposure can lead to respiratory illness in healthy children. Not earning enough income to afford more than sub-standard housing makes it hard to attain better health. Not having more than a high school diploma can make attaining better employment a challenge and prohibit one's ability to attain a higher paying job. Low-wage and part-time jobs often lack full benefits such as affordable health insurance and paid sick leave. The cycle of poverty is real and prevents many from attaining their highest health.

Furthermore, the underlying causes for the inequities in health and the social determinants of health are attributed to racism and discrimination. There is a wealth of data showing that racism and discrimination affect access to education, home mortgage loans, employment, and promotions. It can be shocking for many people to realize that the condition of the spaces where you live, work, and play are largely constrained by your race and ethnicity. But, this realization is important and particularly important for our legislators who make laws that affect how our health insurance, access to health services, transportation, education, employment, and a myriad of other facets critical to our lives and well-being. I am hopeful that if we can educate voters and legislators alike about the underlying root causes of the social determinants of health and the economic and social justice benefits of addressing the determinants, then we have a fighting chance at closing the disparities gaps between so many communities of color throughout our nation.

Before I take us further into this, you may notice that I am using the term health "disparity," and not "health inequity" or "health inequality." The term "health disparity" is often used in much of the public health literature on racial and ethnic groups, in particular since the 2001 and 2003 Institute of Medicine (IOM) reports brought attention to this term. "Health disparities" is also frequently used synonymously with the terms "inequity" or "inequality." The Department of Health and Human Services Secretary's Advisory Committee (SAC) for Healthy People 2020, the nation's 10 year plan to improve the nation's health, convened a subcommittee to define the term "health disparity" as the DHHS realized that lack of clarity on this issue impeded progress towards reducing racial and ethnic disparities and socioeconomic disparities in health and medical care (Braveman et al. 2011). For the purposes of this brief, we will stick with the term "health disparity" and the definition of health disparity as outlined in the US Department of Health and Human Services Healthy People 2020 agenda. DHHS defines a health disparity as

> a particular type of health difference that is closely linked with social, economic, and/or environmental disadvantage. Health disparities adversely affect groups of people who have systematically experienced greater obstacles to health based on their racial or ethnic group; religion; socioeconomic status; gender; age; mental health; cognitive, sensory, or physical disability; sexual orientation or gender identity; geographic location; or other characteristics historically linked to discrimination or exclusion (Department of Health and Human Services (US) 2010).

The term "health disparity" also often includes health care disparities, which refers to differences in the quality and amount of care given to different racial and ethnic groups (Koh et al. 2011).

When health disparities refer to differences, the term "inequity" is sometimes used to signify an ethical judgment (Carter-Pokras and Baquet 2002:427). Margaret Whitehead of the World Health Organization defines "health inequities" as "differences in health, which are not only unnecessary and avoidable but, in addition, are considered unfair and unjust" (Whitehead 1991). Braveman et al. (2011) in *Health Disparities and Health Equity: The Issue is Justice* view health disparities and the determinants of health as metrics for assessing health equity, which they see as "the principle underlying a commitment to reducing disparities in health and its determinants; health equity is social justice in health." Similarly "inequality" denotes a "lack of equality as of opportunity, treatment, or status" (Carter-Pokras and Baquet 2002). In the United States, public health and social science use the term "health disparity" whereas internationally, the terms "inequity" and "inequality" are more commonly used (Carter-Pokras and Baquet 2002). The interviews of legislators that formed the foundation of this research were conducted in Massachusetts and as such, I chose the term, "health disparities," as it was more likely to be familiar with the legislators that I met with. Therefore, throughout the rest of this brief, I will refer to the differences in health outcomes between different groups as "health disparities," but readers should know that the differences are avoidable, unjust, and unfair.

While the health differences are real, great, avoidable, unjust, and unfair, they also have serious financial consequences for not only the people suffering from poor health, but to their communities, businesses, and even the productive capacity of our nation. I am moved to end these differences solely from a social justice standpoint, but I think that it may be the financial savings from closing the dispari-ties gap that hold the greatest promise for advocacy. I briefly mentioned earlier that diseases associated with racial and health disparities affect one's personal produc-tivity and subsequently, the productivity and business outputs of our nation. Additionally, poor health leading to an inability to work leads to decreased tax revenues and a rise in the use of social services. But, how much do these effects cost our businesses and affect our nation's fiscal health? They cost a whopping $8 trillion according to the April 2018 report titled, "The Business Case for Racial Equity: A Strategy for Growth" from the W.K. Kellogg Foundation (WKKF), Altarum, and the report's author, Ani Turner (Turner 2018). The report makes a compelling case for closing the racial equity gap and notes that "by 2050, our coun-try stands to realize an $8 trillion gain in GDP by closing the U.S. racial equity gap" (Turner 2018).

> Convincing data is presented that lay out how closing the racial equity gap can lead to meaningful increases in consumer spending, as well as federal and state/local tax revenues, and decreases in social services spending and health-related costs. For example, in con-sumer spending alone, closing the racial equity gap in the U.S. would generate an additional $109 billion spent on food, $286 billion on housing, $30 billion on apparel, $147 billion on transportation, and $44 billion on entertainment each year. Federal tax revenues would increase by $450 billion and state and local tax revenues would increase by $100 billion annually (Turner 2018).

Faced with numbers like these, I don't see how our legislators would not want to close the racial equity gap. It makes both fiscal and social justice sense. But, based on my interviews with legislators from the Commonwealth of Massachusetts, where a great deal of health reform has served as the basis for national health reform efforts, it seems clear that the dearth of policies looking at closing the racial equity gap, the health disparities gap, and those addressing the social determinants of health is due to a lack of understanding amongst our legislators nationally on health equity.

Now that we have defined health disparities and the importance of eliminating health disparities and inequities, it is fitting to learn from Dr. Georges Benjamin, the Executive Director of the American Public Health Association (APHA). Leading APHA, the only organization that influences federal policy in efforts to improve the health of the public, Dr. Benjamin shares his thoughts on "Becoming the Chief Health Strategist" on public health and politics, advocacy, and coalition building in this first "Notes from the Field."

"Notes from the Field" from Dr. Georges C. Benjamin: Becoming the Chief Health Strategist

Introduction

The overall health of the population of the United States ranks poorly compared to other industrialized nations when looking at a broad set of measures. This is particu-larly of concern when one looks at the fiscal investment made in health of over

$3 trillion a figure almost twice the other high income nations. Efforts are underway to change the national ranking and many believe that part of the problem is the need for clearer leadership to drive a healthiest nation agenda. The concept of a Chief Health Strategist is a leadership function that has caught hold to provide health improvement at the local, state and federal levels. Having someone to provide health leadership is essential if one is to adequately influence public policy that will achieve making the United States a healthier nation.

Public Health and Politics

Government's role in influencing public policy is conceptually for four distinct but often overlapping reasons: First to ensure public safety and welfare, second for economic reasons when there is a market failure, third for moral or ethical reasons, and finally to meet a specific political goal.

Both governmental and nongovernmental public health is practiced through a political lens because it is often the practice of influencing public policy. Any chief health strategist will need to work in a political world to make health happen and many are unclear about how to navigate in a highly political and charged environment. Politics is basically the practice and theory of influencing other people. It also includes the practice of the distribution of power and resources within a given community. It is used to influence public policy goals that government or other entity chooses to do, or not do, to address a particular problem.

The public has an important role in influencing public policy and is an important piece of input. It is however not the only input because public opinion can be skewed because of confirmation bias. It also can be paradoxical and even inconsistent when the facts are not clear or people are poorly informed such as the now famous comment from those that state 'they what government to stay out of their Medicare.' They believe that government involvement would harm Medicare, but are unaware that Medicare is in fact, a government run, single payer, universal health insurance program.

Today, health policy formulation is very complex because of a host of factors including an antigovernment mood, restrained economy, changing demographics, globalization, rapid innovation at many levels, anti-science ideology amongst some leaders and rapid communication through the internet and social media. In addition, the areas of policy difference between political fractions continue to grow to include the role and size of government, taxes and spending, education and the role of the social safety net. In health, specific fault lines exist for family planning (including abortion), environmental protections, education, firearms, and health insurance coverage. In addition these differences often result in a policy stalemate that results in delays in responding at the policy and funding levels. This is complicated by the fact that public health lives in an incongruent environment where a significant need is identified; funding and other resources are delayed in coming often at insufficient levels, for too limited a scope, and for an inadequate period of time. It is also true that the performance expectations continue far beyond the resources and focus of resource allocators allowing the health problems to recur.

In the past public health practitioners have used the political process to advance the public's health. This was true when John Snow convinced skeptical town officials to remove the Broad Street water pump handle in Soho, London in 1854 to stem the Cholera outbreak or, in 1988 when U.S. Surgeon General C. Everett Koop convinced the Reagan Administration to allow him to mail pamphlets on HIV/AIDS to every household in America or, in 2018 when FDA Commissioner Scott Gottlieb aggressively addressed youth access to e-cigarettes over industry objections as a threat to children's health.

In all of these cases these health leaders used a pathway to policy making that put science first to address the health challenges and worked the political process both internally and externally to great success. They engaged the public, tracked public opinion and worked to inform the public to ensure people received factual information to inform their views.

Becoming the Chief Health Strategist

Becoming the chief health strategist means that you cannot wait for others to "set the table" and invite you to it. Defining a health agenda requires a clear understanding of the problems that exist and a prioritization of what needs to be addressed first. This knowledge will help you understand where you want to go. You then need to understand where you have power, influence or authority to meet the goal. It also requires active collaboration because sometimes you will need to lead but often you will need to follow or be in a supportive role when others are best suited to lead.

Leadership requires the uses of three management tools to effect change: power, influence and authority. Power is the ability to influence others, influence is the process of affecting the thoughts, behavior or feeling of others and authority is the legal right to influence others. Your goal as a chief health strategist is to achieve a balance of all three of these management tools. Of the three tools, influence can be the most effective because it can be used to sway both superiors and colleagues where there is no reporting relationship to point of view. It can also inspire subordinates to follow you to achieve your goals. Your goal with influence is to expand the "zone of indifference." The zone of indifference is the range in which others perceive a concept as legitimate and will agree to act upon it favorably without much thought. As a practitioner of public health you should also know where you or another entity has the legal authority to leverage action. Often a health in all policies approach is most helpful to aid in getting action from traditional non-health organizations. It is also important that things are done using good governance principles. That means using the rule of law in a transparent way that allows for participation of affected parties. It is also important to ensure accountability and sustainability of any proposals.

Advocacy

Getting legislators attention is not difficult, even if you are not a campaign contributor. Citizen advocates have enormous value as a bringer of knowledge. You have even more influence if you are their constituent. While national or state based organizations have value to lay out the case for supporting an issue and give policy makers a sense of the level of support for an issue, constituents who actually vote for their elected leaders, can have a larger voice than organizations. The need for citizens advocates to engage elected leaders is essential. One should engage them early and often. Get to know them before you want them to do something. Become a reliable resource to them as they often are in need of factual information of high quality. More importantly, it is essential that you get to know their staff. In local offices the staff usually cover a wide range of issues and cannot possibly be an expert in all of them, here you can be most helpful by bringing your perspective and knowledge base to them. Even in larger offices with a dedicated health staff, the range of health issues is enormous. Never forget that other people from paid lobbyists, political colleagues and other government officials will also be there to give their perspectives on the issues to the policy maker. When their advice is in variance with yours, you have to have a better argument to be successful.

You do not lose your first amendment rights when you become a government employee. You can advocate as a citizen and should do so as appropriate. There are legal issues that do need to be addressed such as the Hatch Act that prevents political activity, but issue advocacy is usually allowed within certain rules. Certain individuals who find themselves in leadership positions do have to navigate the political waters when they have to support a particular administration position and there are clearly times when it is unwise to be publically supporting a particular point of view. Never the less, effective Chief Health Strategist is often able to provide internal leadership within the political structure to effect the favorable outcome of a decision that impacts health.

Of course one never wins all of these battles. When you lose one, just pick yourself up, analyze why you lost and if appropriate try again at a later time. Issues including legislation have their optimal time for passage. In the late 1990's the Governor in Maryland wanted to pass a small program to give health insurance coverage to about 6000 children. This issue was picked because of an emerging community need to expand coverage for children but was one of the last budget items approved for presentation and the health department had not built an effective case for the need. The number was picked because of fiscal limitations as the entire cost would have been born by the state as these children were not eligible for Medicaid. It failed to pass that year. The next year the Federal Children's Health Insurance Program was passed (SCHIP) by Congress and signed into law by President Clinton. SCHIP provided a 60% fiscal federal match to states as an incentive to participating. Maryland passed legislation authorizing coverage for 60,000 children. During the year between legislative sessions, the health department made a compelling health case for children's coverage and had a better case for the return on investment. In this case timing and political will gave the Governor and his health leaders more time to make a better case for support.

Coalition Building

Active collaboration requires listening and building trust, and compromise without appeasement. It also means becoming a skilled communicator as public health problems require complex and sometimes paradoxical messaging; for example, we often have to give a sound public health message that advises people to not use drugs – but also give a harm reduction message that states – if they do, they must use a clean needle and don't share them; or be sexually abstinent but if you do have sexual relations use a condom. Such messages are often difficult to deliver and require making a sound case to persuade. Sound persuasion requires that one knows the evidence, understands the counter arguments and speak to individuals both intellectually and emotionally. It is also important not to be dissuaded or influenced by false choices.

Building a coalition to support the effort is important to ensure sustainability of any effort. It is an essential part of any policy change effort. Coalitions are built by bringing together all interested parties and then coming to agreement on a common goal. Good coalition building requires a good governance approach, the ability to stay focused on an agreed upon goal. It is also important to recognize that some members with an interest may not be willing or able to participate at a given time and the coalition needs to be able to allow individuals or groups to leave without ill feelings. Interests do realign or unalign over time and the best coalitions have the capacity to engage the right individuals or groups at the right time for the right purpose.

Conclusion

Becoming the healthiest nation requires individuals to step up and take responsibility for not only their individual health but the health of their communities. Those in leadership roles must see themselves as the Chief Health Strategist and work to build the case for support for others to see that good health is a community benefit of enormous proportion.

References

Braveman, P., Kumanyika, S., Fielding, J., LaVeist, T., Borrell, L., Manderscheid, R., & Troutman, A. (2011). Health disparities and health equity: The issue is justice. *American Journal of Public Health, 101*(S1), S149–S155.

Budrys, G. (2017). *Unequal health: How inequality contributes to health or illness*. Lanham: Rowman & Littlefield Publishers, Inc.

Carter-Pokras, O., & Baquet, C. (2002). What is a health disparity?. Public Health Reports. (Washington, DC: 1974), 117(5), 426–434.

Centers for Disease Control and Prevention. (2017). National center for chronic disease prevention and health promotion. 2017 National diabetes statistics report: Estimates of diabetes and its burden in the United States; https://www.cdc.gov/diabetes/pdfs/data/statistics/national-diabetes-statistics-report.pdf.

Creanga, A. A., Syverson, C., Seed, K., & Callaghan, W. M. (2017). Pregnancy-related mortality in the United States, 2011–2013. *Obstetrics and Gynecology, 130*(2), 366–373.

Department of Health and Human Services (US). (2010, December). *Healthy people 2020: Framework*. Washington, DC: DHHS.

Health Resources and Services Administration. (2018). Office of health equity. In *Health equity report 2017*. Rockville: U.S. Department of Health and Human Services.

Herbst, J. H., Painter, T. M., Tomlinson, H. L., & Alvarez, M. E. (2014). Evidence-based HIV/STD prevention intervention for black men who have sex with men. *Morbidity and Mortality Weekly Report (MMWR), 63*(1), 21–27.

Kochanek, K. D., Murphy, S. L., Xu, J. Q., & Tejada-Vera, B. (2016). Deaths: Final data for 2014. *National Vital Statistics Reports, 65*(4), 1–121.

Koh, H., Graham, G., & Gllied, S. (2011). Reducing racial and ethnic disparities: The action plan from the Department of Health and Human Services. *Health Affairs, 30*(10), 1822–1829.

Mack, K. (2013). Drug-induced deaths — United States, 1999–2010. *Morbidity and Mortality Weekly Report (MMWR), 62*(03), 161–163.

Mathews, T. J., & MacDorman, M. F. (2013). Infant mortality statistics from the 2009 Period linked birth/infant death data set. *National Vital Statistics Reports, 61*(8), 1–27. Hyattsville: National Centers for Health Statistics.

Mikati, I., Benson, A. F., Luben, T. J., Sacks, J. D., & Richmond-Bryant, J. (2018). Disparities in distribution of particulate matter emission sources by race and poverty status. *American Journal of Public Health, 108*(4), 480–485.

Murphy, S. L., Xu, J. Q., Kochanek, K. D., & Arias, E. (2018). Mortality in the United States, 2017. In *NCHS data brief, no 328*. Hyattsville: National Center for Health Statistics.

Pew Research Center. (2018, July). Income inequality in the U.S. Is rising most rapidly among Asians.

State Health Fact, Poverty Rate by Race/Ethnicity. (2016). Kaiser family foundation. https://www.kff.org/other/state-indicator/poverty-rate-by-raceethnicity/?currentTimeframe=0&selectedDistributions=black&sortModel=%7B%22colId%22:%22Location%22,%22sort%22:%22asc%22%7D.

Turner, A. (2018). The business case for racial equity: A strategy for growth. https://altarum.org/sites/default/files/uploaded-publication-files/WKKellogg_Business-Case-Racial-Equity_National-Report_2018.pdf.

US Census Bureau. (2016). The 2015 American community survey. https://www.census.gov/programs-surveys/acs/.

Whitehead, M. (1991). *The concepts and principles of equity and health* (Vol. 6, pp. 217–228). Copenhagen: WHO/EURO.

Williams, D., & Jackson, P. (2005). Social sources of racial disparities in health. *Health Affairs, 24*(2), 325–334.

Chapter 2
"The More You Know, the Further You'll Go" or What Do Legislators Know About Health Disparities and What Does This Mean for Public Health Advocates?

Notes in the Field

Woolf and Braveman recognize that "although some academics and policy makers understand the health impact of social determinants, the general public and other policymakers do not always recognize that social policy and health policy are intimately linked" (2011). Therefore, a critical link in this issue is the awareness and knowledge key decision makers have about disparities. With greater awareness and knowledge through education, advocates can hope to close the disparities gap. I sought to get a handle on how much do legislators really know about health disparities and realized that examining Massachusetts legislators would provide some important lessons for advocates across our nation because of the many great strides towards health reform and addressing health disparities that have been taken in Massachusetts. McDonough et al. underscore the importance of "states as catalysts for policy change" as "nearly every major health policy initiative considered by Congress in the last 10–15 years was first devised, tested, and improved through state experimentation" (2004).

One can see in Massachusetts how it serves as a model for national health reform. The 2006 health reform law, also known as Chapter 58, in Massachusetts lowered the number of uninsured residents using a combination of subsidized private insurance programs, Medicaid expansion, and an individual mandate requirement. Many public health leaders see Chapter 58 as a road map and example for the 2010 Patient Protection and Affordable Care Act (ACA). The individual mandate, individual insurance markets, and small-group insurance markets of the 2010 ACA stem from the 2006 Massachusetts health reform law. With so much health reform policy coming from Massachusetts, what did these legislators know and understand about health disparities? And what factors affect what they know about health disparities? What can we can learn and possibly replicate in advocacy efforts in other states?

The Massachusetts General Court is the state's lawmaking body and is composed of 200 members that are each elected to serve two-year terms. This bicameral system consists of a 40 member Senate and a 160 member House of Representatives. Interviewing legislators of the 187th Massachusetts General Court provided insight into their levels of awareness and knowledge of health disparities (the dependent variables under study) and in particular, on what variables affect their levels of understanding. Forty-three legislators were chosen for in-person interviews that included both open-ended and forced response questions. The thirty-one legislators that were chosen for the in-person interviews included those who were assigned to the Joint Committee on Health Care Financing or the Joint Public Health Committee. Interviews with twelve legislators who did not serve on these "health-focused" committees were also conducted to allow for a comparison on whether committee membership affected legislative awareness and understanding of health disparities. The legislator's characteristics (the independent variables) included the following:

- Majority race/ethnicity of the legislator
- Committee membership (whether the legislator served on the Health Care Financing Committee, the Public Health Committee, on both committees, or on neither of the health-related committees)
- Highest level of education of the legislator
- Whether the legislator holds a health-related degree
- Party affiliation
- Median household income of the district(s) that the legislator represents
- Legislative office (whether the legislator is a senator or a representative)
- Gender of the legislator
- Tenure in the legislature

The interview questions can be found in Appendix A. The interview began with questions asking about the legislator's district(s), how interested in politics they perceived their constituents to be, and how their constituents voiced their concerns to them. Thereafter, the legislators were asked whether they thought the following statements were true, false, or didn't know for sure to assess for their levels of awareness and knowledge of health disparities:

1. There are differences in the prevalence, incidence, mortality, or burden of diseases or medical conditions that exist among certain population groups in the Massachusetts.
2. Blacks generally fare worse than whites in infant mortality and Latinos fare worse than whites in terms of health insurance coverage.
3. There is strong and consistent data and evidence that links more education with better health.
4. A socioeconomic gradient in health exists.
5. Lower levels of socioeconomic status increase the risk for diseases by increasing stress.

In reading to yourself whether the above statements were true, false, or whether you didn't know for sure, what did you answer? How would your state legislator or Congress member answer them? And in case you weren't sure, the above five statements are sadly, all too true.

Additional questions were asked of legislators regarding how frequently they heard from their constituents, the media, and family and friends about health care costs, health insurance coverage, health disparities, and access to health services. Legislators were also asked to self-rate their own level of awareness of health disparities, and to note where they received their information on health care costs, health insurance coverage, health disparities, and access to health services. Finally, legislators were asked open-ended questions to determine whether they felt they were different from other legislators in how they obtain their health-related information and if so, whether they were felt that they were different from their colleagues in the amount of information that they hear from their constituents, media contacts, or other personal sources. More about how and from where legislators heard about health care costs, health insurance coverage, health disparities, and access to health services and how to effectively voice your concerns and promote your causes to legislators will also be discussed in Chap. 3 on "How to get your legislator's attention."

In analyzing the demographics of the sample of legislators included in this study, the legislators were typical of most state legislatures and Congress. With the wealth of literature on the power of the incumbency effect in campaigns and elections, it was not surprising to see that in this sample, most of the legislators were experienced with service in office of four or more terms (69.8%). The legislators were highly educated with 32.6% of those interviewed holding a master's degree and 27.9% holding a doctoral degree. Also, not surprising for Massachusetts, the majority of the Massachusetts legislature is Democratic and similarly, 88.4% of those interviewed were Democrats. The demographics of the Massachusetts legislature is also largely male and white/non-Hispanic, and similarly, those interviewed for this research study were mostly male (60.5%) and white/non-Hispanic (90.7%).

So, how knowledgeable and aware of health disparities was this mostly male, white/non-Hispanic, and educated sample of legislators? Given the groundbreaking health care legislation in Massachusetts, it was not surprising in assessing the legislators on their knowledge of the five above-mentioned statements on different aspects of health disparities, that nearly every legislator interviewed (95.3%) correctly identified the first statement ("there are differences in the prevalence, incidence, mortality, or burden of diseases or medical conditions that exist among certain population groups in Massachusetts") as true. The fifth statement ("lower levels of socioeconomic status increase the risk for diseases by increasing stress") is a lesser-known aspect of health disparities, yet still 76.6% of the legislators interviewed correctly identified the statement as true. In creating a summary score for disparities awareness for each legislator based on their responses, 58.1% of legislators correctly identified each statement, 14% correctly identified four of the five statements and 27.9% correctly identified two to three statements.

With these results showing legislators who are largely knowledgeable about health disparities, it is interesting to see how their awareness relates to other characteristics such as whether the legislator is a person of color. In this study, we found that a legislator's race/ethnicity and level of awareness of health disparities were independent of each other. Additional analysis also found no relationship between the legislator's health disparities awareness and the following characteristics: the median household income of a legislator's constituency, a legislator's committee membership, a legislator's level of education, the gender of the legislator, whether a legislator was a representative or senator, and whether the legislator held a health-related degree.

Not necessarily surprising for many, especially given the repeated calls from Republican legislators to repeal the Affordable Care Act, this study revealed a statistically significant association for party affiliation with disparities awareness. A majority of Democrats in this study were more knowledgeable and aware of health disparities than the Republicans. Given reviews of the two political party platforms, it makes sense that Democrats would be more aware of health disparities. The 2016 Democratic Party Platform calls for ensuring equality, ending systemic racism, and securing universal health care (Democrats 2016). Much of the platform calls for tackling the many social barriers to health. In contrast, the 2016 Republican Party Platform calls for a repeal of the Affordable Care Act and supports "Consumer Choice" (RNC Communications 2016).

Though not particularly surprising, but interesting given recent calls for a change in our legislatures and more diversity among candidates and lawmakers, the study results showed a statistically significant relationship between the legislator's awareness and knowledge of health disparities and the legislator's tenure in office. Legislators who have served four or more terms were shown to be more knowledgeable about health disparities than those who served for less than four terms. Having worked with a number of organizations advocating for health equity and access to health care within Massachusetts, perhaps the significance of the relationship between tenure in office and disparities awareness is due to the time that advocates and lobbyists spend developing relationships with legislators. The "tenure" could be indicative of the amount of information and education that advocates have given to legislators.

This research showing the importance of party affiliation and tenure also highlight the power that individuals and coalitions have in raising awareness and that this power is key towards successful public health advocacy for health equity. Understanding the linkages between politics and public health and our own individual responsibility for advocacy is important for not only ourselves, but for our communities. With this research on Massachusetts legislators, it is important to note that no matter what state one lives in and how a state has approached public health prevention or eliminating health disparities, members of the public, and in particular, medical and public health professionals must play an important role in public health advocacy. In this next "Notes from the Field," Dr. Julie Graves shares her insider's view from Texas where she served as Regional Medical Director for the Texas Department of State Health Services for the Houston area and across the nation in her roles as a family medicine and public health physician. Whether battling a Zika outbreak or preparing to host the Super Bowl LI, Dr. Graves shares practical advice for medical and public health professionals on how to advocate for healthier communities and how doing so has made her a "better public health physician."

"Notes from the Field" from Dr. Julie Graves: Advocacy for Reducing Health Disparities: A View from Public Health Practice

We hear much about advocacy in public health, often seeing public health organizations hosting advocacy summits and webinars, but because many of us have been taught that politics is not something to engage in (either by family and community, or by concerns about our role while working for a government agency), many with the expertise to influence and contribute to sound public policy are staying quiet. I urge you to speak up, and to do so with a thoughtful plan. Because public health is a governmental function, we'll never establish public health programs or bring "health in all policies" to realization without advocacy. Our nation's health depends on us.

So what is advocacy? Merriam-Webster's online dictionary gives us this definition: the act or process of supporting a cause or proposal. Supporting can happen in many ways and at all stages of the policy-making process, and public health should be involved at every stage. The term advocacy is often used to avoid the term "lobbying." Our dictionary gives us these definitions of lobbying: "to conduct activities aimed at influencing public officials and especially members of a legislative body on legislation; to promote (something, such as a project) or secure the passage of (legislation) by influencing public officials; to attempt to influence or sway (someone, such as a public official) toward a desired action." Because lobbying has legal implications, many who want to influence public policy use the term advocacy to distinguish themselves from paid lobbyists – people hired by a non-governmental organization such as a corporation or political action committee to influence public policy. Most states and municipalities, and the federal government, require registration as a lobbyist if one accepts payment for the activity at all.

Because many in public health are employees of a government agency, they must often adhere to restrictions on lobbying activities, and some interpretations of being paid for the activity include a government salary. This means that in addition to knowing how to stay within the boundaries of law and rule is as important as knowing how to advocate effectively. How to find out the law and rules? In addition to your public health agency government affairs staff, state public health, medical, and nursing associations often can provide guidance, as can state and local government affairs offices. Another good source is your state representative. Legislative staff can be enormously helpful, providing information on current laws and on policies already in process. I encourage every public health professional to know your own representatives at every level – city, county, state, and federal – to know who they are by sight and to meet with their staff, and if possible, meet them in person, and to know their rights and restrictions on meeting with elected representatives with regards to their employer.

Successful advocacy requires an understanding of how public policy – both law and administrative rule – is made. We must recognize that public health is a government function and know how government works, at all levels. I've found it helpful to read and understand the parts of my state constitution that apply to public health. (I found rules on mosquito control districts far from the public health section). Civics education has been downscaled in public education, and in my experience teaching medical students, I've been surprised at how many are not aware of the steps in policy-making. (Or perhaps it's that many younger Americans didn't benefit from Schoolhouse Rock's "I'm Just a Bill" episode – if you haven't seen it, it's worth a view on YouTube at https://www.youtube.com/watch?v=tyeJ55o3El0). I'll admit that even though my Dad taught high school government, I still learned just the basics of policy-making in high school. The real details had to wait until I joined the state medical association and attended committee meetings on legislation and political action and testified at state legislative hearings, and until I took policy and administrative law courses during my graduate public health program.

Advocates must also understand the structure of governments – what the responsibilities and authorities are of cities, counties, and state entities such as legislatures, administrative agencies, and regulatory agencies. Cities and other municipalities have authority over public health matters in many states, while in others the county or state government has jurisdiction. It's important to know what a government entity can do and what they are obligated to do before talking with them about public health interventions.

Effective advocates have a broad view of public health policy. We need a "30,000-foot view," that is, an understanding of larger political and social issues and their impact on public health programs and outcomes. And, we need a detailed understanding of our local and state governments' public health programs, including the history of public health's presence, influence, strategies, wins, and losses, and of our partners such as medical, nursing hospital, and educator associations, the business community such as Chambers of Commerce, and organizations of government leaders (for example, in Texas an association of county governments is a central site for local policy development). So, advocates must do their homework and learn about who is doing advocacy and to whom it should be directed. Talk with your local city and county governments – look for offices of government affairs and get to the know them. They need to know you for their jobs, and you can partner.

Advocates can tap into existing expertise and partner with those with similar missions, both in and out of a public health agency. Many public health or other related government agencies have public affairs or legislative affairs offices staffed by people with passion for and expertise in advocacy for their own agency or city/county, and many of whom can become partners in advocating for policies that benefit the health of their constituents. Other partners I wish public health would work more with are the professional health organizations such as local and state nursing and medical associations. These organizations often work on scope of practice and reimbursement for health services issues, but one strategy they use is to pair an issue that benefits the medical professional with a "white hat" issue that benefits the public health. In Texas, much health and safety legislation has been enacted because nursing and medical associations promoted it. These are our natural partners in promoting public health, and I urge public health professionals to join their other professional organizations and get involved in their legislative and advocacy committees. The relationships formed there provide opportunities to promote sound public health policy and to engage the strength and numbers of these organizations in promoting these policies.

Another fundamental step is to be clear about what public policies you want to support and move forward. A great source of policy information is the American

Public Health Association's policy statement database (at https://www.apha.org/policies-and-advocacy/public-health-policy-statements/policy-database), and your state public health and medical organizations may have similar resources in which you can read rationales and details of policy recommendations. And, it's important to know what the current law is, what policies are in the pipeline, and which have failed in the recent past and won't move forward with the current legislature or city council in place. To learn about how to frame your policy ideas into actionable policy initiatives, read legislation and learn the process. Most states and many local governments have built public on-line data bases of proposed and enacted legislation, and most entities have an on-line administrative code which contains the rules that administrative agencies use to interpret legislation into actionable public health and regulatory policy. Don't be discouraged at first when reading the densely- and often opaquely-written bills and rules. Legislative bills are usually written by a drafting office within the legislature with significant expertise and a common style, and there are likely experienced staff in legislative offices who wrote bills before these drafting offices were established. Your state public health agency may have staff who focus on bill writing and bill analysis. For most in public health, there's not a need to draft a bill, but instead to clarify the policy one wants to enact and its potential impacts on health outcomes and budgets. This means there is also a need to understand budgets at state and local government levels. "Following the money" is a great way to understand legislators' values and possibilities, to know what elected officials are willing to spend tax dollars on. Making the case for public health and reducing health disparities as a cost-effective investment and not merely an expense to taxpayers is something all of us in public health must do if we want to see sound public health policy enacted. We must show the voters, those who lobby and hire lobbyists, and those who run for office that investing in public health gives a return on investment, that it is not a burden, but instead a benefit to taxpayers.

Former US House of Representatives Speaker Tip O'Neill once said, "All politics is local." I believe that this was once the case, but now in the age of social media and polarization of views, politics is now more party-driven even at local levels. This could mean that public health advocates must work with elected officials whose views on many subjects are counter to those of views held by most science-informed public health professionals. The focus on showing return on investment and the cost/benefit ratio of public health services, rather than a focus on improving health for all, has grown from the shift in philosophy of many in government towards privatization and reduction of services in the interest of lowering taxes. This is a challenge for public health, because our interventions are tax-funded and so must be cost-effective in addition to being evidence-based. It is helpful to understand election cycles, and how local, state, and federal elections line up on the calendar. This affects campaign seasons, when elected officials are available for meetings, and when you might run into them at a community event. It's important to know which elections are partisan and which are not. Many city councils are not partisan, while state legislatures can be extremely partisan. It can also be helpful to know who the big campaign contributors are to elected officials you work with. This can inform you of the pressures they get from others on policy issues, and could inform a strategy on partnering with businesses on issues such as points of distribution for medical countermeasures and immunization at work programs. These relationships may provide an opportunity for you to ask these businesses to put in a good word for your public health programs when they meet with elected officials.

Outside of the legislative area there are other opportunities for public health advocacy. Your advice and guidance for physicians, nurses, and others working in the health care arena on the importance of collaborative public health advocacy and on the scientific basis of public health can benefit the community as well as strengthen partnerships. One example is getting important information about outbreaks and changes in disease patterns into the hands of clinicians. Sending one email is usually not enough. What's worked for me is engaging county medical and nursing societies, hospital systems, and provider groups such as large multi-specialty medical clinics and offering to speak at lunches and continuing education events and to write for their newsletters and magazines. During the Zika outbreak over recent years, getting information out to the public took a coordinated approach. As a state health department physician I worked with city and county health officials, vector control departments, and emergency management staff, providing them with sound evidence-based information and working with them to talk to the public whenever I could. Alongside city and county health officials and elected officials, I attended news conferences, town halls with legislators, area-wide conferences and meetings, union meetings, and briefings, and I gave grand rounds and lectures to health professional students and practitioner groups whenever I could. I sent the epidemiologists, nurses, community health experts, and veterinarians in our department out to talk with citizen groups and the media. We developed targeted emails that went out from county medical societies, hospitals, and other organizations with short bullet-point lists of information and links that we believe were more likely to be read than yet another (long, wordy) health department email. By providing user-friendly information, facts, and action steps, and by collaborating with partners, we were able to inform our community effectively and to reach many more people that our budget would usually allow.

A lesson from this Zika outbreak example is that we in public health have things that policy makers need – information and examples. We need to understand that much of public policy is made on anecdote and by appealing to the emotional as well as analytical sides of elected officials. We may need to collaborate with members of the public who have been affected by a public health issue to provide the vignettes that work so well in testimony in public hearings. We need to know the data and how to share it in formats that are specific, give context, and are visually appealing. Public health departments and agencies have the expertise and talent to do this and should use in-person and electronic information sharing as well as look to leveraging social media. It's now important for public health agencies to have social media experts working with health educators and communication experts, and for data and demographic experts to collaborate so that accurate information goes to the public and to policy makers in formats that are visually appealing and understandable. Social media posts can link to public health agency websites that provide more extensive information while getting critical points across succinctly to the wider public and are sure to be noticed by elected officials' press staff. Following elected officials on social media keeps you informed of public policy activities and may result in them following your agency as well!

What about that common fear many have of public speaking? I wonder if many in public health avoid advocacy activities because there's likely a need at some point to speak in public. I recommend practicing speaking in public and in small groups to friendly audiences. If needed, take a toastmaster-type or similar course. One great source for public speaking training for public health professionals is the FEMA (Federal Emergency Management Agency) public information officer (PIO) courses that many emergency management offices offer (https://training.fema.gov/programs/pio/). I took a course taught by the U.S. Coast Guard and another taught by my state's emergency management office. These crisis communication skills have been immensely valuable and broadly applicable, and so have the personal connections I made during those courses. If there's not a group of public health and safety PIOs in your community who meet and share information and learn from experts, set one up. Meeting regularly with PIOs from communities in my region kept me and my agency in the loop during crises and reminded these agencies of public health's commitment to our role in disaster preparedness and response. Since many of these PIOs worked with leaders in their own governments, these relationships helped build bridges and communication pathways for work in other areas. Sometimes the best advocacy for public health is that done by people who aren't in a public health agency. Imagine the effectiveness of emergency management leaders speaking in favor of public health funding!

Another example of a successful advocacy strategy for public health interventions is to find out how local elected officials want communication. When I started as a public health physician and medical director, I met with the county executives and mayors of jurisdictions in my region. During those meetings I brought them a tailored one-page document about the Robert Wood Johnson/University of Wisconsin county health rankings with highlights of things their county was doing well and not-so-well (http://www.countyhealthrankings.org/). The community health professionals in my office prepared easy-to-read graphics from the health ranking reports. For the lower rankings in that county, we suggested solutions – programs that could be implemented to improve that ranking. In those initial meetings I asked the county executives how they preferred to communicate, and I gave them my cell phone number, email, and snail mail addresses. I offered (and some accepted) to text them my cell phone number and asked if I could text them in an emergency. I encouraged them to contact me about public health any time and to bring their local public health staff and authorities into our calls and meetings when appropriate. I was clear that I'd keep their confidentiality and work with them on what information should be made public. The results were strongly positive. One county executive used only Facebook to communicate, so I set up an account just for him. His expertise in using this platform was evident when his county experienced serious flooding, and he livestreamed the view from a helicopter so he could show his constituents where dangerous roads were to be avoided, and to show EMS and police who might need rescue urgently. Later he reached out to me for assistance about a possible food-borne outbreak at a county fair, about vaccines, and about informing his county about Ebola and Zika. Other county executives asked me for guidance about spraying for mosquitoes, about rabies control, and about how to choose a physician to be the local health authority. I asked them for guidance on talking to the state legislators from their counties. When a large-scale tuberculosis testing effort was needed at a school after a prolonged exposure to an active case, the county executive helped me talk with school officials and offered to send law enforcement and emergency management services including paramedics during the testing event to help with traffic and people who might faint when getting blood drawn. The relationships were positive and productive because I started out with information about their county, suggested solutions for them, offered to help and partner with them, and gave them the flexibility to communicate with them in a way that worked for them.

Other helpful partnerships are with local emergency management and law enforcement officials. These public servants are the others who see health dispari-ties in the field and understand as we do in public health the challenges people face every day regarding health and safety. And, we share some responsibilities in disas-ter preparedness and response, so getting to know them is helpful for advocacy as well as for our work in preparedness. Once we had established relationships, we talked about health disparities and disaster response. For example, one state 211 system offers a registry for people with disabilities who have mobility impairment, those who have electric-powered medical equipment, and others so we can plan for evacuations needing specialized equipment and more time in a disaster. Epidemiologists and local government agencies with GIS (geographic information system) expertise can collaborate to identify evacuation routes and transportation routes to medical shelters. These collaborations provide paths for educating these partners about health disparities and solutions to these disparities. And, as my friend and former colleague Dr. David Persse, Director of Emergency Management and Health Authority for the City of Houston often says, "You shouldn't be handing out business cards at the disaster." He's right. Getting to know our partners and getting contact information into our cell phones can make big differences when that disaster does come. We were fortunate in Houston to host Super Bowl LI in 2017 and to have during the previous year many tabletop exercises and gatherings with preparedness and response teams from the region facilitated and hosted by the National Football League and by federal agencies. During that year the connections and sharing of contact information and plans has made the Houston area safer and was so benefi-cial during the successful responses to Hurricane Harvey later in 2017.

School nurses are willing and capable partners for health information and action. During Zika, school nurses in our region thought up innovative efforts such as teaching schoolchildren to be "standing water detectives" at school and encouraging them to do this at home with their families, and teaching about mosquito repellent and programs for public funding for pregnant women to get free repellent. Public health nurses provided continuing education programs for school nurses that included ways to contact programs and materials for teaching about public health in their communities. It's a goal of mine to get public health officials and education leaders talking with each other about how we can incorporate the public health information that everyone needs to have into all schoolchildren's curriculum.

Community engagement by public health experts is immensely beneficial in laying the groundwork for advocacy efforts in these communities. One example is to send your (almost always) personable public health veterinarians into the community to educate and advise. I've been fortunate to work with veterinarians who could calm parents worried about rabies exposure from bats in a school building and engage a neighborhood in which a canine rabies case was identified. I've learned communication skills that are broadly applicable from these vets – they seem to have a knack for calming upset animals and people alike. Another example comes from an early-career community health professional who noted that in his community with much and rapid growth and lots of construction that many workers were brought in from other towns and were staying in hotels away from family. The local bars got lots of business, but there was an increase in driving while intoxicated arrests and automobile crashes on weekend nights. This public health professional went to bar owners and asked if they would offer free soft drinks to a designated driver in each group at their bars on weekends – with success. A reduction in arrests and car wrecks was a welcome result. This was advocacy at its best: effective, and it gave local business owners a specific action to take that improved public health. It was a joy to discuss with local government officials and law enforcement leaders about this program before it started, and even better to talk about its success afterwards.

I have a few other ideas. I wonder if restaurant inspectors could provide information on healthy foods, especially to establishments in food deserts. And for coastal communities, could oyster bed inspectors link workers to hepatitis A vaccines, perhaps inviting the immunization nurses out to vaccinate from time to time. I encourage you to dream big about ways you can bring public health into the community and invite elected officials to learn about your work and the benefit public health agencies bring to communities.

My last advice on advocacy is to say "yes" when possible. When community groups, professional organizations, clinics, hospitals, schools, unions, and elected officials call the health department to ask a question or request help, say "yes." In my case, a call from U.S. Soccer resulted in me getting to brief the U.S. Women's Olympic Soccer Team about Zika before the Rio de Janiero games. (Yes, I got to meet these amazing athletes and they are all super smart and nice!) Calls from elected officials resulted in me getting to provide information about outbreaks on local television and radio outlets. Give out your cell phone number and thank people for calling. Offer to speak and to provide information and materials. Advocacy is important at the level of elected official, and it's equally important in communities and at the one-to-one level. You'll know it's working when you get invitations like the one I cherish still, to an event hosted by a Member of Congress at which free immunizations were provided to members of a low-income community who were experiencing transportation barriers to public clinics and at which she stayed for 5 h, talking with every constituent who wanted time (and often a selfie) with her.

(It was Rep. Sheila Jackson Lee.) Advocacy can be daunting at first, but working with elected officials and our partners who care about healthy, thriving communities has been rewarding and meaningful, and made me a better public health physician. I hope you'll come on in – the (inspected by sanitarians) water's fine!

References

Braveman, P., Kumanyika, S., Fielding, J., LaVeist, T., Borrell, L., Manderscheid, R., & Troutman, A. (2011). Health disparities and health equity: The issue is justice. *American Journal of Public Health, 101*(S1), S149–S155.

Democrats. (2016). 2016 Democratic national platform. Retrieved from https://democrats.org/about/party-platform/. Accessed 20 Feb 2019.

McDonough, J., Gibbs, B., Scott-Harris, J., Kronebusch, Navarro, A., & Taylor, K. (2004, June). A state policy agenda to eliminate racial and ethnic health disparities. The commonwealth fund. http://www.commonwealthfund.org/programs/minority/mcdonough_statepolicyagenda_746.pdf. Accessed 1 Apr 2013.

RNC Communications. (2016). The 2016 Republican party platform. Retrieved from https://www.gop.com/the-2016-republican-party-platform/. Accessed on 20 Feb 2019.

Chapter 3
How to Get Your Legislator's Attention

In Chap. 2, we learned that party affiliation and tenure in office were statistically significant for legislators' disparities awareness with Democrats and those who served four or more terms in office to be more aware of health disparities. We also learned of the important roles that physicians and public health professionals play in influencing health policy and community health. With this data and the wisdom of Dr. Graves, we know that it's important to engage members of all political parties in movements for health equity and to ensure that newer legislators must also be made aware of the critical connections between the social determinants of health and population health. January 3, 2019 saw the swearing in of the most diverse class of freshman lawmakers in Congress. If one is serious about ensuring that all who reside in the U.S. have the ability to live to their full potential, then Republican lawmakers and this new class of lawmakers needs to hear the calls for health equity.

Recent marches and protests such as the Women's March and the March for Science, show that people from all across the nation are trying to make their voices heard. Large, national organizations to smaller grassroots and non-profit organizations are all trying to get the attention of both policymakers, voters, and would-be voters. The *Washington Post* noted that the 2017 Women's March was "likely the largest single-day demonstration in recorded U.S. history" (Chenoweth and Pressman 2017) with estimates between 3,267,134 and 5,246,670 people marching. Data from the Pew Research Center (DeSilver 2018) show that the 116th Congress is more diverse than before and comprised of nearly 24% women in the House of Representatives and 25% in the Senate, yet still does not reflect the diversity of our nation's population.

This recent increase in diversity in Congress has largely been attributed to an increase in women and in particular, in women of color running for office. In many ways, I see this as a sign that many people are fed up with not seeing the needs and concerns of their communities being addressed by their government. Or, as U.S. Representative Ayanna Pressley who was recently sworn into the 116th Congress, said "change can't wait." As a public health practitioner with a deep

© The Author(s), under exclusive license to Springer Nature Switzerland AG 2020   23
C. Chanyasulkit, *Successful Public Health Advocacy*, SpringerBriefs in Public Health, https://doi.org/10.1007/978-3-030-30288-7_3

interest in closing the disparities gaps, it poignant to have heard Pressley repeat throughout her campaign that "the people closest to the pain should be closest to the power."

Despite this increase of female candidates in local, state, and federal elections, a quick look at Congress reveals how unrepresentative our government still is. Therefore, efforts to educate our legislators and draw their attention to evidence-based science and policy are still sorely needed if we are truly to live a society where all people have the ability to live to their full potential. But, what is the best way to make your voice heard? How can we move from evidence-based research to action? I call my senators and representatives. I write emails to them. I tweet. Does it make a difference? How are you reaching out to your legislators? And why do you reach out to them in the manner that you do? Have you found it to be an effective way of advocating? Do your legislators respond positively to you?

Not wanting to continue to spin my wheels and looking to learn more about how aware legislators are of health disparities, I also asked legislators about how frequently they heard from their constituents, media contacts, and family and friends on health care costs, health insurance coverage, access to health services, and health disparities and whether the outreach affected their level of awareness of health disparities. Although the results of my research cannot be generalized to all legislators, it was interesting to learn that they heard so frequently from different sources about health care. Asking the legislators to rate their frequency of communication from their constituents as never, sometimes, or all the time regarding health care costs, health insurance coverage, access to health services, and health disparities, my interview research revealed that on average, legislators heard nearly all the time from constituents on health care costs, but only sometimes on health insurance coverage, access to health services, and health disparities.

In seeing how frequently legislators heard from their media contacts, the interviews revealed that on average, legislators sometimes heard from them on health care costs, health insurance coverage, and access to health services, and health disparities. Similarly, legislators sometimes heard from their friends and family on health care costs, health insurance coverage, and access to health services, and less so on health disparities. To move the nation towards health equity and to eliminate the widening health disparities gaps, we need to make sure that legislators hear from advocates ALL the time and not just "sometimes."

But, don't just take it from me. In our next "Notes from the Field," Senator Cynthia Creem of Massachusetts explains why it is important for legislators to hear from their constituents and why this persistent and unwavering outreach is important to passing laws. Then, you'll gather time-tested tips on how to attract your legislator's attention from former legislative staffer Stefanie Coxe, who provides Learn to Lobby in-person and online courses on lobbying and activism through Nexus Werx LLC, her activism and lobbying training and consulting company.

"Notes from the Field" from Senator Cynthia Stone Creem

When I was first elected to the State Senate by the people of Newton, Brookline and Wellesley, my upbringing and my background as an attorney led me to my passion for progressive legislation to promote social and economic justice. I have been fortunate since then to have the support of my politically involved constituency to help me set priorities toward these goals.

Throughout my public career, first as a City of Newton Alderman and Chair of the Board, and later as an elected Governor's Councilor, I have been guided by the principle of fairness. When I became an attorney, women were treated differently in the legal profession. In order to obtain a license to practice, I was subjected to an interview where I was grilled about my plans to have children, and knowing I could be denied a license I did not reveal that I was already pregnant with my first child. It was a humiliating and inappropriate use of power. And it became a defining moment in my legislative career. No individual should have to face discrimination on account of gender, race, ethnicity, religion, age, sexual orientation or gender identity.

For those who serve as legislators, patience is a necessity. It is often repeated that "politics is a process" and that legislation moves slowly – often taking three or more sessions before sufficient consensus is built. When legislators are unfamiliar with an issue, or when it is technically complex, there is a learning curve. There are several, if not hundreds, of issue areas, and over 6000 bills to evaluate as well as yearly budgets. This is where advocates can be especially helpful. Emails, phone calls and office visits all educate representatives and staff. It is also important for individuals to join groups working together across districts, because these often have more resources (like printing flyers and arranging rallies). Associations can help educate the public at large through letter campaigns and media outreach.

Most bills do not get signed into law. Therefore it is also important, if difficult, for a legislator to communicate disappointing news to advocates and the public. Every bill encounters roadblocks, which can be procedural, as when House and Senate Committee chairs disagree on how to move a bill forward, or policy-driven, where members are deeply divided on whether something should become law. There may be legal questions on conflicting laws, or questions from the administration about implementation. As an example, sometimes there is a good idea for a new policy, like all-day kindergarten (which I support). But local school committees also know that without more state funding, adding these classes means they will have to cut their education budgets elsewhere. Sometimes a good policy can stall out, or become a pilot program instead. Mandatory full-day kindergarten has been debated for many years, but a consistent revenue stream has never been identified and sufficient funding has never been set aside to implement this worthy policy.

Legislation can also sometimes come about because of a single constituent. One law I am proud of sponsoring came as the result of a meeting I had with a constituent about her food allergies. She could not safely eat out because the way foods were prepared at restaurants did not take into account whether customers had any allergies. Ingredient lists were missing or incomplete, and servers did not know how to address customer questions appropriately. My constituent and I knew it was unfair for the many people with severe food allergies, who often missed social opportunities or had to pack separate foods. We worked together to draft legislation requiring restaurant training for servers, and promoting food allergy awareness.

This bill required collaboration with multiple outside organizations, including restaurant and food allergy associations, as well as educating legislators and staff on the importance of this issue. The concept may seem simple, but it still took several years to become law.

Legislation can also succeed when a critical mass of public opinion shifts, and credit is often due to the innumerable individuals and organizations who have worked alongside legislators to change policy. In 2018, after many years when I and others had filed and re-filed criminal justice reform legislation, a comprehensive bill became law; among its provisions, it will reduce the number of people incarcerated for petty and non-violent crimes, provide meaningful alternative paths to work and school, and reform policies on solitary confinement and juvenile justice.

It's important to remember that there are multiple perspectives to consider and every proposal should be carefully weighed. That is why legislators need to hear from their constituents, through email, in person, or by phone, so we can learn the variety of opinions and the specifics on how a new law may impact their life. That is why we need individuals to reach out and educate legislators as important issues arise.

"Notes from the Field" from Stefanie Coxe

Introduction

Closing knowledge gap between lawmakers and public health experts begins with the understanding that *legislators are generalists* who rely on outside interests (you) for specifics.

It's simply not possible for them to know everything about every issue, so it's incumbent upon advocates to educate them. And like a teenager toggling between multiple phone apps, getting and holding their attention is difficult; lawmakers have dozens, if not more, competing requests from different interests group each week. Each advocate is equally convinced theirs is the most important issue and the correct policy.

In order to successfully transfer knowledge and pass policies, advocates must rise to the top of a very large pile of competing requests. This is accomplished by becoming known and trusted through building relationships and political capital, along with preparing for, executing, and following up on advocacy engagements in a manner that conveys credibility.

Building Relationships and Political Capital

Political relationships are like any other relationship. The more someone knows and trusts you, the more likely they are to go out on a limb for you. The more lopsided the relationship, the harder it is to make inroads. And when a relationship is non-existent, it makes walking into a lawmaker's office and asking them to do something (advocacy) awkward and more challenging than it needs to be.

Building Relationships

When I first started out in politics, I was lucky enough to meet a hero of mine – and a great public health advocate – the late Senator Ted Kennedy (D-Massachusetts). As I approached him, the senator said, "hi, nice to see you again." I just nodded. I didn't want to tell him we'd never met.

Later, I became friends with a staffer for another politician who was active on the national and international stage. This person laughingly relayed an anecdote that should give you insight into how many people politicians meet. This staffer was one of many working in the district and accompanied the politician to speak at a community event. After he spoke, the politician made the rounds, shaking hands with various local dignitaries and constituents. After 20 or 30 mins of this, the politician approached his staffer…and introduced himself!

My friend looked down sheepishly and replied in a hushed tone, "sir…I work for you".

Politicians meet and greet constituents, lobbyists, reporters, staffers, and many, many, more people each week. They become a blur. Most of the time, people are asking them for things.

The best lobbyists and citizen-advocates relationship-build with lawmakers prior to and in between those encounters. Advocates should never dismiss the efficacy of simply saying 'hello' to officials and their staff. Whether stopping by their office, attending a public event, or going to their district office hours, networking in the political sphere is as important as in the business world.

Whenever I run into a member of the Massachusetts Legislature, even if I think they know me, I remind them how we know each other or where we last saw each other. I give them the grace and cover of a prompt so the neurons can fire and they can make the connection. In addition to reminding them, doing this engenders a feeling of familiarity and appreciation that they don't have to spend the next few minutes making small talk while searching their memory for how they know me. With relationship building, the goal is for them to associate you with positive feelings so they'll be more willing to go out on a limb.

Building Political Capital

Often, lawmakers only hear from an advocate when they need something. If they've consistently been supportive but received nothing in return, it begins to feel a bit toxic and one-sided. Now, most legislators have no expectation of campaign contributions or campaign work (though that never hurts). But everyone likes someone who makes their job easier and lawmakers are more receptive to asks from those who've done so consistently.

In the "real world," we use currency to trade the things we have for the things we need. In the political world, the currency is one of favors, or "horse-trading." As a public health advocate, you are an information resource, an authority, and a validator. Use these roles to build *political capital* by providing decision-makers with "talking points" and local statistics from their district.

Part of the challenge of being a public official is that – while it's next to impossible to have depth of knowledge across a wide breadth of topics – people still expect it. Some of the best politicians are those whose knowledge is a mile wide and an inch deep; but they make the most of that inch, absorbing relevant statistics, stories, and talking points.

As a subject matter expert, you can compile information that will help them paint an informed picture when discussing public health issues in their district and with the press. For example, when an AIDS support group proposes a needle exchange in their town and panicked parents call demanding opposition, a lawmaker who has been proactively informed not only of the proven efficacy of needle exchanges but also of the prevalence of substance use disorders in their district, will most likely handle questions from the public and the media differently than an uninformed lawmaker. But note that in order to be helpful and digestible, the information should be conveyed on a one-page document, using clear problem and solution statements and bullet form.

Delivering this information means more than dropping off a one-pager. Information that's not associated with a face and a name (relationship-building) tends to go towards the bottom of the pile. Lawmakers and their staff need the high-level pitch of why they should pay attention. An explanation that you're offering evergreen information intended to be useful to them will spark their interest. "I understand that you meet regularly with family groups in your district. I think these stats could really impress them."

Have you ever noticed how many organizations have a "legislator of the year" award? Maybe you've been in a lawmaker's office and been taken aback by the number of plaques and awards on the wall behind their desk? Why is that?

One of the most important "jobs" of an elected official is to stay in office. Otherwise, they can't keep helping people. To fulfill that job, they need to show the voters in their district they're doing a great job advocating for them. Awards and the ensuing press releases and social media posts provide those officials with a way to convey to their constituents just how hard they're working.

Another tool to build political capital is sending in a positive letter to the editor of the local newspaper in their district, praising them for their hard work. Offering social media kudos can also help, particularly if you have constituents in their district 'authoring' or sharing the praise.

Just be sure the topic is something they want publicly advertised rather than a topic they'd prefer flies under the radar. I'm member of the political committee for Planned Parenthood Advocacy Fund of Massachusetts. I'm thrilled when a lawmaker is vocally supportive of, for example, the Healthy Youth Act, which provides a framework for comprehensive sex education. But I also recognize that some parts of our state are more conservative than others and in order to be re-elected and continue to help us pass important legislation like Healthy Youth, we may not want to draw local attention to their support of a locally controversial issue. When in doubt, ask their aide if a letter to the editor would be helpful.

The Anatomy of the Ask

Lobbying decision-makers involves far more than simply showing up at their offices on a lobby day. To maximize success, there is a certain degree of preparation and follow-up required, along with using wisely those precious few moments you have with a lawmaker or their staffer.

Decide What the *Specific Ask* Is

Decide what *specifically* you're going to ask the lawmaker to do. The vaguer the ask, the smaller the chance it will be acted on. Again, decision-makers face competing requests from many, many other people. They'll act on the asks that most align with their values and interests, but also the ones that are the most *actionable*.

Ensuring policy makers understand that there are racial and economic disparities in public health outcomes is incredibly important. But as a public health advocate, it should be the beginning of your advocacy rather than the end point.

Going back to the idea that lawmakers are generalists, if they are provided with data showing disparities alone, without a specific policy recommendation, they're likely to walk away bewildered, wondering *"what do they want me to do with this; I'm not an expert, they are."*

Asks need to be concrete. Even interactions with a regulatory agency filled with policy experts needs to go beyond asking that racial and economic disparities are factored into new policies. Government is slow, reactionary, and bureaucratic. The advocate's job is to push for the inclusion or exclusion of specific policy recommendations on multiple proposals. If you ask a policy maker to "be on the lookout" for an issue or include a recommendation in every new public health proposal they work on, they won't. The next person rising to the top of the pile will take their attention away.

How specific do you need to be?

Most advocates ask their elected officials to "support House Bill 1234."

Unfortunately, it's easy for a politician to wriggle out of a support/oppose ask.

What if your bill never makes it to the House floor for a vote? In that case, the legislator may never have a chance to support or oppose the bill. They can say, "oh yes, I supported H.1234," but what does that actually mean?

If you don't make a specific ask, you have no metric for measuring your lawmaker's actions. Support or oppose is vague and amorphous.

I encourage you to reach out to a health advocacy organization that specializes in the issue and get their advice about what would be most helpful. It may mean asking the lawmaker to:

- Co-sponsor a bill
- Write/or sign onto a letter to the Committee chairman and Ranking member
- Personally speak to a key decision maker such as the Speaker
- Sign onto an amendment

Once you have a specific ask, you'll better be able to hold their feet to the fire and have better data on where you stand with that lawmaker.

Do Your Homework

When I was in my early twenties, I went to D.C. for a conference along with a group from my community. Before we left, some members of the organization asked us to advocate for specific budget priorities with our Member of Congress and Senators.

When it came time to meet with our Congressman, each of us got an issue to ask for. Well, I was completely overwhelmed at that point and didn't bother doing any homework on what it was I was asking for. I just went in with my talking points.

Our Congressman sat down at a small table in his office with us and when my turn to make an ask came up, using my notes, I asked him to support funding for a juvenile diversion program. I went on for a moment about how important it was. Slowly, a smile came across his face.

Eventually, he asked me, "do you know who started that program?" Clueless, I shook my head. He smiled again and said, "me, when I was district attorney."

Let me tell you, I turned several shades of red. It's pretty embarrassing to ask someone who championed an issue to support it. Now, the Congressman was great and I'm sure the fact I was so young factored into his assessment of my credibility.

But It Did Damage My Credibility It made me look inexperienced and clueless – because I was! That could have been so easily avoided, had I taken a few easy steps. Take the time to research if the lawmaker is on the record in the newspaper opposing the bill you're meeting on or if she's a well-known champion of it.

No matter how obscure the issue, chances are there's an advocacy organization professionally lobbying on it, which can help you with your advocacy planning. They should have this information at their fingertips. If they don't it may be a sign they're not effective.

Effective Messaging

"Framing"an issue for each decision-maker you meet with is critical to winning them over. Each lawmaker has a set of pet projects and areas of specialty. For example, communities of color, particularly African-Americans, have a higher health burden from air pollution compared to the overall population. Say you are courting the vote of a lawmaker who is a housing advocate. Reference the history of zoning and housing development, which lead those communities to be housed in more hazardous areas (it's not a coincidence that the Lower 9th Ward in New Orleans got hit the hardest in Katrina). If the legislator is an environmentalist, frame it as an important statistic to back up the need for reduced emissions (or, bonus points, as a way for that lawmaker to win over another legislator who cares about public health issues on an environmental vote). That goes, too, for say, the Chair of the Transportation committee. "Mr. Chairman, I know how much you care about investing in public transportation. I'm right there with you. In fact, folks in the African-American community are experiencing shockingly high health effects from all this congestion on the roadways."

Much of advocacy is knowing what not to say. A Democrat will certainly be persuaded by an equity argument, but few Republicans respond well to social justice warriors. Instead, since health disparities affect productivity levels, decreasing tax revenues and increasing the use of social services, a suburban Republican will respond to key phrases like "closing the disparity gap will yield financial savings for public programs."

Think about it from the old sales line, "what's in it for me." This is usually directly linked to the local statistics. If a politician or their staff realize that they could be looking at a lot of unhappy voters in their district, alarm bells are going to go off. How could this impact their chances at re-election? Could someone do a tv ad saying their vote hurt constituents?

Lastly, consider the power of storytelling in your messaging. When I worked for a Member of Congress, he supported local community health centers. But it wasn't until he went on a tour of one of them and met actual constituents impacted by the center and heard their story that he became a true champion. After that, he was telling everyone he met – in Congress and in the District – about what good work this health center was doing and why funding was so critical.

Putting a human face to an issue dramatically increases your ability to sway an elected official. You're touching their humanity through storytelling. Storytelling is one of the things that makes a politician override the political calculus. Even if something is going to cost him politically – either in DC or in the District – if he is truly moved and convinced he's doing the right thing for his district, he'll take the risk. To the extent it's practical try to have a story about or from a constituent for each lawmaker. Storytelling that touches the heart while also hitting the "what's in it for me" button is a winning combination.

The One-Pager or "Leave-Behind" Document

Concise delivery of an ask is communicated with a simple message, limited statistics, and a realistic request provided on a "one-pager." And I do mean one-page. As a staffer, anytime I was handed an interesting looking study, packet, or actual book on an issue, it went in a pile of "things I'll look at when I have time" only to be thrown in the recycle bin 3 months later on an organizing spree. My boss and I understood, digested, and retained complex information when it was explained in simple form – preferably bullets. In science and academia, statistics, citations, and detail are valued. In politics, brevity and distillation of an issue are prized. Trust me, if they want more, they'll ask for it.

Things to include:

- Program/Bill name, line-item/bill number
- If you're asking them to co-sponsor something, don't forget to name the lead sponsor. And while you're at it, include your name and contact info!
- Information about who and how many (ballpark) people who will be impacted (preferably people in their district) and why it's important.

This one-pager can also used as your "cheat sheet" to make sure you the have details jotted down in the event of a temporary brain freeze. (Lobbying can be intimidating; it's okay to have notes!)

Get on Their Schedule

If you're meeting in person with the lawmaker or their staff – either in their Capitol office or the District office – try to schedule a 10 min meeting ahead of time. Call to confirm the meeting and, for pity's sake, if you're running late, call and let them know. Don't be afraid to meet with an aide if they cancel last minute. It happens all the time due to last minute votes and staff are the ones who do most of the work anyway.

Perfect Your Elevator Speech

An elevator speech is literally what you can say if you're going from the 10th floor to the 1st with the lawmaker: who you are, where you're from (organization), what you're concerned about (specific issue) and why it's important.

If the legislator doesn't understand what you want in less than a minute, your credibility and ability to communicate decreases. The important thing with an elevator speech is to keep it high level. Tell them what it is you're asking for, what problem it's fixing (or what gain it's creating), why it's important to his/her district, and–if it's funding– how it will be sustained. The details, whether it be bill nuances or personal stories, can be addressed later in the conversation. You just want to grab their attention by showing them you're a credible advocate and letting them know what you want.

Plan on limiting your time to 5–10 min. If they choose to extend the conversation, great. But plan on getting everything across in 5 min or less.

Whether in-person or over the phone, the conversation should typically go something like this:

- **Identify yourself.** "Hi, I'm Stefanie Coxe. I'm a constituent from Cambridge."
- **Ask to speak** with the elected official or aide responsible for the subject matter. (If you're calling an office, expect that you'll be speaking with staff. Again, that's okay. They can be your best advocate).

- **Let them know what you'd like to discuss** – in one line. For example, "I'd like to talk to you about health disparities."
- **Ask them a question** to engage them: "Senator Smith is sponsoring legislation to improve public health outcomes. Have you heard of it?"
- **Use your framing and storytelling**
- **Ask if the elected official has taken a position.** If not, ask if you can connect with them later on once they've had a chance to consider. Get their aide's extension or email.
- **Make sure they have all your contact info**. This also applies if you get a voicemail.
- **Thank them** for taking the time to hear you out.

Follow-Up, Follow-Up, Follow-Up

A week or two after your meeting or phone call, make a pleasant call to the aide asking if their boss has had a chance to consider your request or take an action promised in the meeting.

- **Identify yourself** and remind them of the previous conversation
- If they haven't made a decision, tell them you'll **follow-up again** in a few weeks
- Make a **note in your calendar** to call again

At the conclusion of the advocacy, thank them. Thank yous help because they're rare. They build warm feelings (and relationships). And they make lawmakers and staff feel appreciated.

Send them a note thanking them for taking the time to meet with you. Thank their aide. If they do as you ask, take it further. If this is an issue they would want made public, send a letter to the editor and/or a social media shout out. If they've really hit the ball out of the park, give them an award. All these actions rebuild political capital and keep the relationship going.

Conclusion

Effective advocacy comes down to understanding where decision-makers are coming from and putting yourself in their shoes. Once you understand how much they are being pulled in competing directions and that they want to stay in office so they can keep helping people, logical engagement follows:

- Get their attention and rise to the top of the pile by establishing familiarity and making their lives easier (build relationships and political capital)
- Take the time to prepare by deciding on a specific ask, researching the lawmaker's history on the issue, determining how you'll message the ask, and scheduling the meeting

- Practice your elevator speech and have a one-pager ready to go
- Take the time follow-up, both on the ask and with thank yous

The cycle starts all over again after a win. Advocacy is rarely "done." There's always a new issue to champion or oppose, a new lawmaker in office to relationship-build with, and political capital to be built. Regular, rather than infrequent, engagement, will position you to more effectively advocate for public health policy goals and the people you represent.

References

Chenoweth, E., & Pressman, J. (2017, February 7). This is what we learned by counting the women's marches. *The Washington Post*. Retrieved from https://www.washingtonpost.com/news/monkey-cage/wp/2017/02/07/this-is-what-we-learned-by-counting-the-womens-marches/?noredirect=on&utm_term=.5d8fa497128d.

DeSilver, D. (2018, December 18). A record number of women will be serving in the New Congress. *Pew Research Center*. Retrieved from http://www.pewresearch.org/fact-tank/2018/12/18/record-number-women-in-congress/.

Chapter 4
If at First You Don't Succeed…

Try, Try Again I have served in various leadership roles including as an advocate for the needs and concerns of women and Asian Americans as a gubernatorial appointee to the Massachusetts Commission on the Status of Women and the Asian American Commission, as Co-Chair of the Brookline Commission for Women, and as an Executive Board member of the American Public Health Association. These roles have made me see the truth in the often used expression of "if at first you don't succeed, try, try again." I have also learned that change is hard. Change is very hard. But, change is possible.

The gender wage gap is a wonderful example of where I recently saw that "change is charge, but change is possible" happen in Massachusetts. In 2009, former Governor Deval Patrick first appointed me to the Massachusetts Commission on the Status of Women (MCSW). The purpose of the Commission is "to advance women and girls toward full equity in all areas of life and to promote rights and opportunities for all women and girls" (Massachusetts Commission on the Status of Women 2019). With this purpose, the MCSW focused on passing legislation that attempted to close this wage gap and began efforts at addressing the lack of pay equity since 2005. It was during my years as a Commissioner on the MCSW that I learned more deeply about the wage gap and more importantly, about how to advocate for change.

In 1945, Massachusetts became the first state in the nation to pass an equal pay law. In 1963, the first federal equal pay law was passed, but unfortunately, the gender pay gap continues to persist. 2017 data reveal that full-time women working year-round in the United States are paid about 80% of what men were paid (Fontenot et al. 2018). This 20% wage gap has real consequences not only for the working women, but also for their families, children, and communities as research shows that over 40% of mothers with children under the age of 18 are their families' primary or sole breadwinners (Glynn 2016). This wage gap also continues to affect women and their families throughout their lives.

C. Chanyasulkit, *Successful Public Health Advocacy*, SpringerBriefs in Public Health, https://doi.org/10.1007/978-3-030-30288-7_4

As of 2017, women are estimated to earn 80 cents for every dollar that white men earn. Drilling further into the wage gap reveals the pernicious effects of racism and discrimination. 2017 data for full-time working Hispanic, Latina, American Indian, Alaska Native, black, African American, and Native Hawaiian or other Pacific Islander (NHPI) women reveal that they continue to have lower median annual earnings when compared with non-Hispanic white and Asian women (U.S. Census Bureau 2018). Hispanic and Latina women earn 53% of what a white man earns, while black and African American women earn 61% of a white man's earnings (U.S. Census Bureau 2018). The gender wage gap exists in nearly every occupation regardless of a woman's level of education and grows wider as women get older – threatening their economic security and that of their households. Income affects one's ability to gain an education, access health services, attain employment that pays a living wage, and is therefore an important social determinant of health.

Despite early setbacks and opposition, the MCSW continued to advocate for ending wage discrimination and closing the pay gap. The MCSW, the Massachusetts chapter of the National Organization for Women (MassNOW), and the Women's Bar Association (WBA) co-founded the Equal Pay Coalition in 2014. The coalition drafted legislation (S.2119, An Act to Establish Pay Equity) and advocated tirelessly for equal pay. After many forums, outreach, letters to the editor, meetings with business organization, and hearings, Governor Charlie Baker signed "An Act to Establish Pay Equity" into law on August 1, 2016. The law's provisions attempt to tackle the many factors that drive the gender wage gap. This first in the nation law prohibits asking for an applicant's salary history during the hiring process. This not only helps women, but also helps men. Businesses that conduct a good faith audit of their own pay practices and make efforts to correct any salary discrepancies will be provided protections as well. This law also allows for employees to discuss their salaries and compensation without fear of retaliation – a practice that is good for both men and women. Not only my hope, but that of many other advocates, is that this law will serve as model for other states throughout our nation and that state by state, women and families can earn the pay they deserve and thereby, opportunities to lead healthier lives.

As this brief concludes with a final "Notes from the Field," I want to take a moment to acknowledge that it can take a long time, a great amount of data, significant outreach, strong coalition-building, and strategic messaging to build a movement. But, the time and persistence can and does lead to real and sustained change. We see this change in our daily lives. The many public health achievements of motor vehicle safety, reduction in tobacco use, vaccinations, and fluoridation of water are a few of many examples where evidence-based research and continued efforts at advocacy have led to movements that have resulted in great improvements in the overall health and well-being our world.

Wanting to leave you with hope and optimism that change is possible and to give you more tips on how to affect change, this brief concludes with an important example of fighting for change and for reproductive justice as seen in the efforts of the Planned Parenthood Advocacy Fund of Massachusetts that works "to advance access to sexual health care and defend reproductive rights" (Planned Parenthood). In this final "Notes from the Field," Dr. Jen Childs-Roshak, President of Planned Parenthood Advocacy Fund of Massachusetts, and Tricia Wajda, Vice President of

External Affairs of Planned Parenthood Advocacy Fund of Massachusetts, reflect on the 2017–2018 state legislative agenda in Massachusetts and detail how PPAF seized the moment to protect access to reproductive health care and improve sexual and reproductive health outcomes for Massachusetts residents. Be sure to pay special attention to their "key takeaways" which can help you as you develop and implement effective public health advocacy campaigns in your community.

"Notes from the Field" from Dr. Jennifer Childs-Roshak and Tricia Wajda of the Planned Parenthood Advocacy Fund of Massachusetts: "Taking Action in the Trump Era: How the Planned Parenthood Advocacy Fund of Massachusetts Protected and Expanded Reproductive Health, Rights, and Freedoms"

The Planned Parenthood Advocacy Fund of Massachusetts' Legislative Priorities in the 2017–2018 Legislative Agenda

At the start of the 2017–2018 legislative session in Massachusetts, we at the Planned Parenthood Advocacy Fund of Massachusetts recognized that the national political environment had created a new sense of urgency to lead the country in passing proactive policies that safeguard reproductive rights. PPAF crafted a bold, legislative agenda that addressed national threats to Planned Parenthood patients' health and rights and dismantled persisting barriers to care.

With our supporters, coalition partners, and ally lawmakers, PPAF launched and executed several multilayered advocacy campaigns to protect Massachusetts residents from the Trump-Pence administration's attacks and to improve reproductive health, rights and freedoms in the Commonwealth. Our legislative successes were clear (Fig. 4.1).

Fig. 4.1 State policies PPAF supported and ultimately passed in the 2017–2018 legislative session

Our 2017–2018 Legislative Successes Included:

1. An Act Relative to Advancing Contraception Coverage and Economic Security (ACCESS)

Signed Into Law November 2017

The Contraceptive ACCESS law codifies the Affordable Care Act's guarantee of no copay birth control coverage into state law, protecting birth control access from federal assaults. Furthermore, the law proactively expands access to birth control by requiring coverage of a 12 month supply of birth control in a single dispensing and establishes no cost-sharing for over-the-counter emergency contraception purchased without a prescription (Fig. 4.2).

2. An Act to Protect Access to Confidential Healthcare (PATCH)

Signed Into Law April 2018

The PATCH law closed an alarming loophole in patient privacy protections. Before this law, insurers routinely sent Explanations of Benefits (EOBs) to the primary subscriber of the insurance plan, detailing the services received by dependents on their plan. This jeopardized the confidentiality of individuals on their spouse's insurance and young adults on their parents' insurance plans. Now, confidential health care information is not shared with anyone other than the patient when multiple people are on the same insurance plan. Individuals can request how and to whom an EOB is sent and, if no payment is due, to opt-out of EOBs. The EOBs now use generic terms such as "office visit" rather than detailed service descriptions that could violate patient confidentiality.

3. An Act Negating Archaic Statutes Targeting Young Women (NASTY Women)

Signed Into Law July 2018

The NASTY Women law repealed archaic laws enacted to criminalize abortion and contraception and make reproductive health services inaccessible. While these outdated laws were rendered unconstitutional and largely unenforceable, the retirement of United States Supreme Court Justice Kennedy made clear that Roe v. Wade was

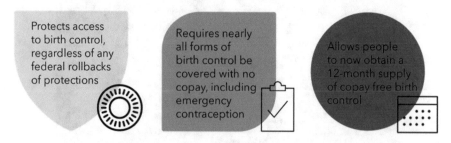

Fig. 4.2 The provisions of the *Contraceptive ACCESS Law*

at risk. By repealing these unnecessary and harmful laws, Massachusetts reaffirmed its own commitment to reproductive rights and access to safe, legal abortion.

4. An Act Relative to Healthy Youth

Passed in the Senate July 2017; Not Brought to a Vote in the House
The Healthy Youth Act seeks to set a basic standard for sex education in Massachusetts by ensuring that a public school choosing to teach sex education selects a curriculum that is medically accurate, age-appropriate, LGBTQ-inclusive, and comprehensive. A truly comprehensive curriculum teaches the benefits of delaying sex, how to prevent unintended pregnancy and sexually transmitted infections, and how to understand and respect consent. Without this legislation, young people remain vulnerable to the harmful, inaccurate abstinence-only-until-marriage programs supported by the Trump-Pence administration.

5. An Act Establishing a Family and Medical Leave and Temporary Disability Insurance Program

Signed Into Law June 2018
The law establishing Paid Family and Medical Leave (PFML) helps ensure no one has to choose between paying their bills and caring for a sick family member or a new child. The law provides benefits for workers to take up to 12 weeks of family care leave – to care for a new child or address a family medical emergency – and up to 26 weeks of leave to take care of their own health. With this policy in place, workers, particularly those who have low-income or are single parents, will be better able to care for themselves and their families.

6. An Act Establishing the Massachusetts Pregnant Workers Fairness Act

Signed Into Law July 2017
The Pregnant Workers Fairness law protects pregnant and breastfeeding workers from discrimination and ensures they are provided reasonable accommodations to stay healthy and keep their jobs. In the past, an employee could be forced to continue working without basic accommodations, risking their own health and the health of their pregnancy, or face losing their job. Under this law, workers cannot be required to take unpaid leave when reasonable accommodations would enable them to continue working. This law ensures everyone, no matter their career, can decide to become a parent in a supportive, healthy work environment.

Best Practices for Legislative Advocacy

PPAF launched several multilayered advocacy campaigns related to our legislative priorities, strategically rooted in a compelling narrative about the Trump-Pence administration and its determination to undermine many of our communities' health and rights on a national level. We understood that our state policies could shield Massachusetts from these federal attacks. Using PPAF's advocacy around the Contraceptive ACCESS Law as a case study, we will share several of our best practices learned from our legislative successes:

1. Create Urgency by Leveraging the National Threats on Our Health and Rights

The multiple attempts by the Trump administration to repeal the Affordable Care Act (ACA) and undermine coverage for no copay birth control made clear what was at stake: 1.4 million women in Massachusetts could lose access to no copay birth control.

By educating lawmakers, reporters, and our supporters about the immediate risk to Massachusetts women, we created an urgent local call to action: pass the Contraceptive ACCESS bill to protect our residents from these attacks.

Within weeks of the Trump administration officially rolling back ACA birth control protections, the ACCESS bill passed the Massachusetts House of Representatives 140–16 and unanimously passed the Massachusetts Senate, 27–0. Massachusetts Governor Baker signed the ACCESS bill into law on November 20, 2017. Responding to the groundswell support for the bill that PPAF's advocacy campaign generated, Massachusetts became the first state to act after President Trump gutted federal birth control coverage protections.

Key Takeaway: *Create a sense of urgency for all of your prospective audiences (lawmakers, the media, supporters, etc.) Explain why NOW is the right time for the State House to pass your policy proposal.*

2. Educate Lawmakers About ACCESS

At the start of the new legislative session, on the heels of President Trump's inauguration and the National Women's March, PPAF and our coalition partners organized a Sexual Health Lobby Day event in support of the bill and other key sexual and reproductive health priorities. Over 500 supporters attended the Lobby Day, met with their lawmakers, and educated them about the need for protecting and expanding access to affordable birth control (Fig. 4.3).

PPAF amassed early and widespread support for the Contraceptive ACCESS bill, garnering an impressive number of legislative cosponsors, and securing hearing testimonies from 25 diverse organizations and 150 patients, providers and supporters.

Throughout the legislative session, PPAF took the time to meet one-on-one with key allies and champions to educate them about the provisions of the bill, the national threats to care, and the urgent need for action (Fig. 4.4).

Key Takeaway: *Create a strong in-house presence for your bill and work to educate and make in-roads with as many lawmakers as you can, on both sides of the aisle.*

Fig. 4.3 PPAF youth activists attending the 2017 Sexual Health Lobby Day at the Massachusetts State House

Fig. 4.4 PPAF's *Contraceptive ACCESS* advocacy work

3. Forge Unexpected Partnerships

To demonstrate broad support for the bill and leverage our collective power, PPAF collaborated with our coalition partners, including NARAL Pro-Choice Massachusetts, the ACLU of Massachusetts, and several other ally organizations.

In addition, we forged a strategic partnership with a seemingly unlikely ally: insurers. Specifically, we partnered with the Massachusetts Association of Health Plans and Blue Cross Blue Shield, two organizations well respected within the Massachusetts State House. Initially, both organizations had concerns about certain provisions of the bill and how it would impact insurance providers. PPAF and the insurance plans met several times, addressed our collective concerns and priorities, and ultimately reached an agreement on the bill. Side-by-side, we spoke together at a press conference held immediately before a legislative hearing where we each testified in support the Contraceptive ACCESS bill. Creating strategic partnerships with these two organizations and resolving differences before the legislative hearing was instrumental in convincing lawmakers to move the policy forward and, inevitably, helped earn the support from the governor.

Key Takeaway: *Build broad and diverse support for your legislative priorities through strategic partnerships.*

4. Center Patient and Supporter Voices

We leveraged our Health Center Advocacy Program to elevate and center Planned Parenthood patient voices in our ACCESS campaign. In all of Planned Parenthood League of Massachusetts' five health centers across the state, the Advocacy Fund hosts an advocacy station where patients can sign a petition, share their story, and get involved with our advocacy work. As part of our larger strategy, we launched a petition drive encouraging patients to share why access to affordable birth control matters to them – and to contact their lawmakers in support of the bill.

In addition to our patient advocacy strategy, we launched several online and offline strategies to organize our supporter base around the Contraceptive ACCESS bill. We created digital tools allowing supporters to easily share their support to their lawmakers and on social media. We encouraged supporters to show up to the bill hearing, community forums, and other advocacy events. For supporters who weren't able to attend in person, we Facebook livestreamed key events like the bill hearing and signing and used #ACCESSBillMA to curate live updates around the bill. Several times throughout the campaign, we were able to generate vocal digital support from activists, ally organizations and lawmakers, as demonstrated by #ACCESSBillMA trending on Twitter.

Key Takeaways: *Center and elevate the voices of those most impacted by the policies you are advocating for. Utilize your advocacy campaign to create opportunities for new activists to join the larger movement.*

5. Engage the Media

From the day after President Trump was elected up until the ACCESS bill was signed into law, we launched a proactive media campaign regularly educating reporters and editorial boards about the threat to birth control access. Members of the media covered our Sexual Health Lobby Day, the ACCESS bill's legislative hearing, along with other key peaks during the legislative advocacy campaign. Our strategic media campaign resulted in 230 media hits mentioning our advocacy work, including three supportive editorials of the Contraceptive ACCESS bill, and national coverage in outlets like Vox, Newsweek, and NPR's Here and Now.

Key Takeaway: *Incorporate a comprehensive media strategy early on into your advocacy campaign – and leverage key peaks to create momentum, public support and urgency for your bill.*

Conclusion

On November 20th, 2017, 10 months after we initially launched our Contraceptive ACCESS campaign, we stood next to Massachusetts Governor Charlie Baker as he signed the Contraceptive ACCESS bill into law, guaranteeing 1.4 million

Fig. 4.5 Governor Baker signing the *Contraceptive ACCESS Bill* into law at the Massachusetts State House

Massachusetts women continued and expanded access to no copay birth control. Through our advocacy campaign, we activated a powerful movement centered on reproductive freedom, economic justice, and a shared belief that affordable contraception access is imperative for breaking down systemic barriers to education success, employment gains and positive health outcomes (Fig. 4.5).

While we saw tremendous success here, it's important to note this was the second legislative session we filed the Contraceptive ACCESS bill. Other priorities of ours, including our sex education policy the Healthy Youth Act, still hasn't become law despite 8 years of fierce advocacy. Working on proactive policies that help close health disparities isn't easy – it requires strategic and persistent effort. However, by leveraging every tool in your toolkit and paving a clear path forward, public health gains can be made.

References

Fontenot, K., Semega, J., & Kollar, M. (2018). *Income and poverty in the United States: 2017.* Washington: U.S. Census Bureau.

Glynn, S. J. (2016). *Breadwinning mothers are increasingly the U.S. norm.* Washington, DC: Center for American Progress. www.americanprogress.org/issues/women/reports/2016/12/19/295203/breadwinningmothers-are-increasingly-the-u-s-norm.

Massachusetts Commission on the Status of Women. (2019). Mass.gov, www.mass.gov/orgs/massachusetts-commission-on-the-status-of-women.

U.S. Census Bureau. (2018). American community survey 1-year estimates. Data tables available from American FactFinder, factfinder.census.gov.

Appendix A: Interview Questions for Legislators

1. Tell me a little bit about your district.

   a. What is its most distinguishing characteristic (the aspect that sets it apart from other districts)?
   b. What kinds of people live there—How interested are they in politics? (A5 point response scale)
   5 = Very interested, 4 = interested, 3 = Neutral, 2 = Not very interested, 1 = no interest.
   c. How do they usually communicate with you? For example, what percentage of their communications to you is from each type? [Most legislators ranked the options or named their top option.]

   - Telephone call
   - Email
   - Office visit
   - Postal mail

   To be read by Student Investigator to the legislator (in italics below) prior to questions 2–6:

   With these next few questions, I'm trying to find out what people know about health disparities. I am going to read a series of statements and for each one, I want you to tell me if it is true, false, or if you don't know for sure about the topic.

   I hope the answers will add to the literature on decision-making and information processing. So, it's important for you to tell me if you don't know about the topic that I ask about. I prefer that you don't guess at your answers. Actually, I expect that there will be some topics that you don't know about.

2. There are differences in the prevalence, incidence, mortality, or burden of diseases or medical conditions that exist among certain population groups in the Massachusetts. Is this true, false, or whether don't you know for sure?

C. Chanyasulkit, *Successful Public Health Advocacy*, SpringerBriefs in Public Health, https://doi.org/10.1007/978-3-030-30288-7

3. Blacks generally fare worse than whites in infant mortality and Latinos fare worse than whites in terms of health insurance coverage. Is this true, false, or whether don't you know for sure?

4. There is strong and consistent data and evidence that links more education with better health. Is this true, false, or whether don't you know for sure?

5. A socioeconomic gradient in health exists across the entire socioeconomic distribution and does not just adversely affect the people at the bottom. Is this true, false, or whether don't you know for sure?

6. Lower levels of socioeconomic status increase the risk for diseases by increasing stress. Is this true, false, or whether don't you know for sure?

7. Using a 0-10 scale of importance where a zero indicates no importance whatsoever and a ten indicates the highest level of importance, **how important do you think each of the following policy areas is for legislative action in 2011–2012?**

IMPORTANCE LEVEL

		NOT AT ALL	SOME	HIGHEST
a.	Roads and highways	0 1 2	3 4 5	6 7 8 9 10
b.	Public Transportation	0 1 2	3 4 5	6 7 8 9 10
c.	Crime	0 1 2	3 4 5	6 7 8 9 10
d.	K-12 Education	0 1 2	3 4 5	6 7 8 9 10
e.	Higher Education	0 1 2	3 4 5	6 7 8 9 10
f.	Jobs and unemployment	0 1 2	3 4 5	6 7 8 9 10
g.	Taxes	0 1 2	3 4 5	6 7 8 9 10
h.	Health care costs	0 1 2	3 4 5	6 7 8 9 10
i.	Health insurance coverage	0 1 2	3 4 5	6 7 8 9 10
j.	Access to health services	0 1 2	3 4 5	6 7 8 9 10
k.	Health disparities	0 1 2	3 4 5	6 7 8 9 10

8. And, using a 0 to 10 scale again where now a 0 indicates obtaining no information in this session from any source on these issues and a 10 indicates obtaining a lot or a great deal of information from any source, how much communication/information do you obtain on the following issues?

AMOUNT OF COMMUNICATIONS LEVEL

		NONE	SOME	A LOT/A GREAT DEAL
a.	Roads and highways	0 1 2	3 4 5	6 7 8 9 10
b.	Public Transportation	0 1 2	3 4 5	6 7 8 9 10
c.	Crime	0 1 2	3 4 5	6 7 8 9 10
d.	K-12 Education	0 1 2	3 4 5	6 7 8 9 10
e.	Higher Education	0 1 2	3 4 5	6 7 8 9 10
f.	Jobs and unemployment	0 1 2	3 4 5	6 7 8 9 10

g.	Taxes	0 1 2 3 4 5 6 7 8 9 10
h.	Health care costs	0 1 2 3 4 5 6 7 8 9 10
i.	Health insurance coverage	0 1 2 3 4 5 6 7 8 9 10
j.	Access to health services	0 1 2 3 4 5 6 7 8 9 10
k.	Health disparities	0 1 2 3 4 5 6 7 8 9 10

9. Now, using a 0 to 10 scale where now a 0 indicates never obtaining information in this session from your constituents and a 10 indicates obtaining information from your constituents all the time, how often do you obtain information about the following from your constituents? How often in this session do you obtain information about health care costs, health insurance coverage, access to health services, and health disparities from your constituents?

FREQUENCY OF COMMUNICATIONS LEVEL FROM CONSTITUENTS

		NEVER	SOMETIMES	ALL THE TIME
a.	Health care costs	0 1 2	3 4 5	6 7 8 9 10
b.	Health insurance coverage	0 1 2	3 4 5	6 7 8 9 10
c.	Access to health services	0 1 2	3 4 5	6 7 8 9 10
d.	Health disparities	0 1 2	3 4 5	6 7 8 9 10

10. Now, using a 0 to 10 scale where now a 0 indicates never obtaining information in this session from media contacts and a 10 indicates obtaining information from media contacts all the time, how often do you obtain information about the following from the media?

**FREQUENCY OF COMMUNICATIONS LEVEL FROM
MEDIA CONTACTS**

		NEVER	SOMETIMES	ALL THE TIME
a.	Health care costs	0 1 2	3 4 5	6 7 8 9 10
b.	Health insurance coverage	0 1 2	3 4 5	6 7 8 9 10
c.	Access to health services	0 1 2	3 4 5	6 7 8 9 10
d.	Health disparities	0 1 2	3 4 5	6 7 8 9 10

11. Now, using a 0 to 10 scale where now a 0 indicates never obtaining information in this session from family and friends and a 10 indicates obtaining information from family and friends all the time, how often do you obtain information about the following from the your family and friends?

FREQUENCY OF COMMUNICATIONS LEVEL FROM FAMILY
& FRIENDS (PERSONAL EXPERIENCES)

		NEVER	SOMETIMES	ALL THE TIME
a.	Health care costs	0 1 2	3 4 5	6 7 8 9 10
b.	Health insurance coverage	0 1 2	3 4 5	6 7 8 9 10
c.	Access to health services	0 1 2	3 4 5	6 7 8 9 10
d.	Health disparities	0 1 2	3 4 5	6 7 8 9 10

12. After thinking about the amount and frequency of communication that you receive from various sources, what would you say your level of awareness is on say some issue like health disparities. Awareness being defined by the Merriam-Webster Dictionary as "having or showing realization, perception, or knowledge." Using a 0–10 scale of awareness where a zero indicates no awareness whatsoever and a ten indicates the highest level of awareness, how aware would you say you are about health disparities?

AWARENESS LEVEL FOR HEALTH DISPARITIES

	NONE AT ALL	SOME	A LOT/A GREAT DEAL
Health Disparities	0 1 2	3 4 5	6 7 8 9 10

13. For each of these health issues, I also know that you frequently use sources other than people to obtain information about these issues, so I'll now ask about those. Using a similar scale where now a 0 indicates obtaining no information in this session from popular magazines and a 10 indicates obtaining a lot or a great deal of information, how much information do you obtain about the following issues from popular magazines?

AMOUNT OF INFORMATION OBTAINED FROM
POPULAR MAGAZINES

		NONE	SOME	A LOT/A GREAT DEAL
a.	Health care costs	0 1 2	3 4 5	6 7 8 9 10
b.	Health insurance coverage	0 1 2	3 4 5	6 7 8 9 10
c.	Access to health services	0 1 2	3 4 5	6 7 8 9 10
d.	Health disparities	0 1 2	3 4 5	6 7 8 9 10

14. How much information do you obtain about the following issues from newspapers?

AMOUNT OF INFORMATION OBTAINED FROM
NEWSPAPERS (ONLINE OR PRINT)

		NONE	SOME	A LOT/A GREAT DEAL
a.	Health care costs	0 1 2	3 4 5	6 7 8 9 10
b.	Health insurance coverage	0 1 2	3 4 5	6 7 8 9 10
c.	Access to health services	0 1 2	3 4 5	6 7 8 9 10
d.	Health disparities	0 1 2	3 4 5	6 7 8 9 10

15. How much information do you obtain about the following issues from television?

AMOUNT OF INFORMATION OBTAINED FROM TELEVISION

		NONE	SOME	A LOT/A GREAT DEAL
a.	Health care costs	0 1 2	3 4 5	6 7 8 9 10
b.	Health insurance coverage	0 1 2	3 4 5	6 7 8 9 10
c.	Access to health services	0 1 2	3 4 5	6 7 8 9 10
d.	Health disparities	0 1 2	3 4 5	6 7 8 9 10

16. How much information do you obtain about the following issues from radio?

AMOUNT OF INFORMATION OBTAINED FROM RADIO

		NONE	SOME	A LOT/A GREAT DEAL
a.	Health care costs	0 1 2	3 4 5	6 7 8 9 10
b.	Health insurance coverage	0 1 2	3 4 5	6 7 8 9 10
c.	Access to health services	0 1 2	3 4 5	6 7 8 9 10
d.	Health disparities	0 1 2	3 4 5	6 7 8 9 10

17. How much information do you obtain about the following issues from the internet?

AMOUNT OF INFORMATION OBTAINED FROM THE INTERNET

		NONE	SOME	A LOT/A GREAT DEAL
a.	Health care costs	0 1 2	3 4 5	6 7 8 9 10
b.	Health insurance coverage	0 1 2	3 4 5	6 7 8 9 10
c.	Access to health services	0 1 2	3 4 5	6 7 8 9 10
d.	Health disparities	0 1 2	3 4 5	6 7 8 9 10

18. Do you think you are different than other legislators here in the Commonwealth in the amount you obtain from these sources (constituents, media contacts, personal experiences with family and friends)?

___Yes
___No

If Yes, how are you different in the amount that you hear from your constituents?
From media contacts?
From other personal sources?

19. What in your opinion is the greatest problem in Massachusetts in health care?

20. In response to their answer to question #19, "Is it something that you think the Commonwealth should deal with?"

Index

A
Advocacy, 22
    community engagement, 21
    definition, 15
    disparities gap, 5
    effective, 33
    Hatch Act, 8
    individual responsibility, 14
    legislative, 39–42
    organization, 29, 30
    party affiliation and tenure, 14
    PPAF, 37
    in public health, 15
    public health interventions, 19
    successful, 15
Affordable Care Act (ACA), 11, 14, 38, 40
African-American infants, 2
Air pollution, 2
American Public Health Association's policy
    statement database, 16–17
Authority, 7, 16, 28

B
Bills, 17, 25, 26, 29, 30, 32, 39–43

C
Chief Health Strategist, 6–9
Civics education, 15
Coalition building, 9, 36
Communication, 46–48
Constituents, 8, 12, 13, 24–28, 31
Costs, 5, 13, 17, 24
Currency, 27

D
Disaster preparedness, 19, 20
Discrimination, 3, 25, 36

E
Equal pay, 35, 36

F
Federal Children's Health Insurance
    Program, 8
FEMA (Federal Emergency Management
    Agency), 19
"Following the money", 17
Follow-up, 29, 33, 34
Framing, 30, 33

G
Gender wage gap, 35
Genetic differences, 3
Global maternal mortality, 1

H
Hatch Act, 8
Health care disparities, 4
Health differences, 1, 4
Health disparities, 1
    awareness and knowledge, 12, 14
    definition, 4
    and disaster response, 20
    interviewing legislators, 12
    knowledgeable and aware, 13

Health disparities (*cont.*)
　media contacts, 24
　on racial and ethnic groups, 3, 4
　statistics, 1, 2
Health inequalities, 4
Health inequities, 3–5
Health insurance coverage, 46
Health policy, 6, 11, 16, 17
Health strategist, 5–9
Healthy Youth Act, 28, 39
HIV/AIDS mortality, 2
HIV prevalence, 1
Housing, 3, 5, 30

I
Immunizations, 18, 21
Income, 2
Inequality, 4
Influence, 7, 15

J
Jobs, 28

L
Latino adults, 2
Leadership, 6–8, 35
Legislation, 8, 13, 15–17, 25, 26, 33, 36, 39
Legislative advocacy, 39–42
Legislative bills, 17
Legislators
　attention, 8, 24
　characteristics, 12
　"following the money", 17
　generalists, 26
　health disparities, 13
　interview questions, 12, 13, 45, 49
　interview research, 24
　interviews, 4
　Massachusetts, 14
　racial equity gap, 5
　state legislatures and Congress, 13
　tenure, 14
Life expectancy, 1
Lobbying
　and activism, 24
　and citizen-advocates relationship-build, 27
　decision-makers, 29
　definition, 15
　legal implications, 15
　public health, 15

M
Massachusetts Commission on the Status of
　　Women (MCSW), 35, 36
Massachusetts General Court, 11
Media, 6, 13, 17, 18, 24, 25, 28, 33,
　　40, 42
Messaging, 9, 31, 36

N
Negating Archaic Statutes Targeting Young
　　Women (NASTY Women), 38

P
Paid Family and Medical Leave
　　(PFML), 39
Partnerships, 18, 20, 41
Party affiliation, 12, 14, 23
Patience, 25
Pay equity, 35, 36
Planned Parenthood Advocacy Fund (PPAF),
　　37, 39–41
Policy, 6, 7, 11, 15–18
Policy areas, 46
Political capital, 33, 34
　and building relationships, 26
　currency, 27
　information, 28
　social media kudos, 28
Politics, 6, 8, 12, 17, 25
Poverty, 2, 3
Power, 7, 14
Protect Access to Confidential Healthcare
　　(PATCH), 38
Public health, 6–7, 15
Public information officer (PIO), 19
Public policy, 6

R
Racial equity gap, 5
Racism, 3, 36
Relationships, 14, 16, 18–20, 26,
　　27, 33
Reproductive rights, 36, 37, 39

S
School nurses, 20
Social determinants of health, 3, 5, 11,
　　23, 36
Social justice, 3–5

Social services, 3, 5, 31
Specific policy recommendation, 29
Storytelling, 31, 33
Strategy, 36, 39, 41, 42

T
Tenure, 12, 14, 23

W
Women's March, 23

Z
Zika, 14, 18, 20, 21
Zip code, 3
Zone of indifference, 7

Printed in the United States
By Bookmasters